GEOGRAPHY
Tourism & Leisure

EUROPEAN COMMUNITY

UNITED KINGDOM OF
GREAT BRITAIN
AND NORTHERN IRELAND

Derek Buttivant

BLACKIE

GEOGRAPHY
Tourism & Leisure

Blackie & Son Ltd
Bishopbriggs, Glasgow G64 2NZ
7 Leicester Place, London WC2H 7BP

British Library Cataloguing in Publication Data
Buttivant, Derek
Geography : tourism and leisure
1. Tourism, Geographical aspects
I. Title
338. 4791

ISBN 0-216-92895-8

Printed in Great Britain by Scotprint Ltd., Musselburgh

Contents

Introduction

TO TEACHERS AND STUDENTS

Just as the economic importance of the tourism and leisure industry is increasing, so is the interest among young people in the wide variety of careers available in the industry. Fundamental to success in almost every branch of the tourism business is a sound geographical awareness.

In *Geography: The Basics*, the companion volume to this book, emphasis was placed on locational knowledge and skills. In this book, the student is introduced to the language, knowledge and specific skills needed as a foundation for vocational qualifications in the tourism and leisure field. Specifically, *Geography: Tourism and Leisure* covers the requirements of the Associated Examining Board's Basic Test (Special) in Geography for Tourism and Leisure but the material will be found equally relevant to other introductory courses such as BTEC courses.

There is no suggestion that this book (or any book) can cover every destination and every set of circumstances. Neither does it set out to train travel agents or couriers. Its purpose is to introduce tourism as a specific kind of geography and to encourage the reader to apply geographical skills and knowledge to a variety of realistic situations.

RESOURCES

Fortunately there is no shortage of travel and tourism brochures and leaflets readily (and freely) available. In addition to the holiday brochures obtainable from travel agents, there are leaflets produced by tourist attractions, regional and national publications available from tourist offices and timetables available from transport operators. A collection of these materials will supplement and provide resources for exercises in this book and will help stimulate student interest. Atlas and other maps will be helpful as students need to become familiar with different styles and scales and to relate one source of information to another. Travel articles from newspapers and magazines provide a further rich source of supporting material while *Prestel* carries up-to-date information for those with access to the service. A more limited source of travel and tourism information can be obtained through *Ceefax* and *Oracle*, the free teletext services on television.

What is Tourism ?

There was a time when only the very wealthy travelled for pleasure. Today nearly everyone is a tourist at some time or other.

You do not have to pay for an expensive overseas holiday in order to be a tourist. Any time you make a journey, however short, to visit a place for pleasure, you are a tourist. Sometimes the term 'leisure' seems more appropriate than tourism: a trip to the theatre or sports centre, for example. Nevertheless, more and more people spend increasing amounts of time on tourism and leisure. Why is this?

There are three main reasons:
  More time
  More money
  Easier travel.

TIME

- Ask some adults you know how many days holiday they have each year. (Remember to include public holidays too.)
- Ask the same people how many hours they work.

While many people still work very hard and some work quite long hours it is unlikely that you will find many who regularly work six or even seven days a week or who have less than about four weeks holiday. Compare the answers to your questions with the information in Figs. 1 and 2.

Fig. 1 Weekly hours of work, 1961–1987

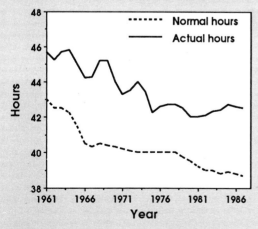

Source Dept of Employ. (Social Trends 19, 1989)

Fig. 2 Annual holiday entitlement, 1961–1987

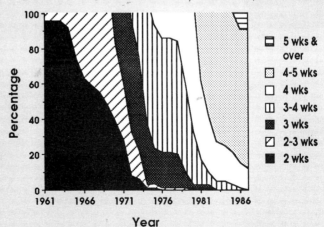

Source Dept of Employ. (Social Trends 19, 1989)

An English seaside resort in the 1930s

Not many years ago almost everyone had only two weeks' paid holiday from work each year and many people could not afford to go away from home on holiday. If they did go away it was usually to the seaside not too far away from home. Today, increasing numbers of people take two or more holidays each year and often travel much further from home. Fig. 3 gives some information about numbers of holidays taken.

- What changes do you notice between 1971 and 1987 as shown in Fig. 3?

As well as holidays spent away from home, many people now enjoy day visits to places of interest, the coast and the countryside. Although these people do not use overnight accommodation they nevertheless add to the overall numbers of tourists and are an important part of the tourism industry.

This, as we have seen already, is partly because people have more hours available for leisure each week, partly because they have more money to spend and partly because improved transport facilities—especially car ownership—allow them to reach more places more easily.

Figs. 3a & b *Number of holidays taken by people in Britain a) 1971, b) 1987*

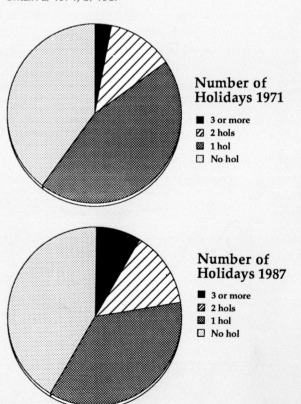

Number of Holidays 1971

- ■ 3 or more
- ▨ 2 hols
- ▦ 1 hol
- ▢ No hol

Number of Holidays 1987

- ■ 3 or more
- ▨ 2 hols
- ▦ 1 hol
- ▢ No hol

Many people go to visit friends and relatives and become holidaymakers or tourists at the same time. These people, too, do not make use of holiday accommodation but represent a considerable number of additional visitors in an area.

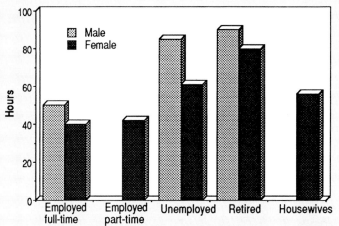

Fig. 4 Leisure time available in Great Britain in a typical week, 1987

Source Henley Centre for Forecasting (Social Trends 19, 1989)

- Can you explain the different amounts of leisure time enjoyed by different groups of people?
- Why is it that the people with most leisure time available are not always able to make the fullest use of it? (Think about the various groups of people shown in Fig. 4.)
- Ask among your friends and list the places they have visited recently on days out.

A noticeboard showing some of the activities on offer at the Aviemore Centre

MONEY

Because so many more people are travelling and visiting for leisure purposes there are now many more facilities provided for them but holidays, days out and the use of these facilities can be expensive. So do people generally have more money to spend on tourism and leisure than they used to?

Wage comparisons

In 1938 average earnings were £2.66 per week.

In 1948 average earnings were £5.87 per week.

Today, most people earn between £100 and £200 per week with many people earning considerably more.

Of course, prices were also much lower in the 1930s and '40s but, even so, people today have a better standard of living and can afford to spend more on leisure activities including holidays. On average, people in Britain now spend just over 5% of their income on holidays—so someone earning £200 a week (about £10,000 a year) might spend £500 on holidays. Remember that many families have more than one person bringing home wages.

An indication of the importance of tourism in the lives of British people is given by the amount of money which is spent on it. In 1987 £14,250 million were spent on tourism, only slightly less than on clothes and shoes (£17,800 million) and fuel, power and petrol (£18,720 million). People spent less on vehicles (£13,560 million) and much less on furniture (£4,880 million) than they did on holidays.

TRAVEL FACILITIES

It is in the speed and ease of travel that the third explanation can be found for the increase in tourism.

Journeys within countries and journeys overseas have been transformed in the second half of the twentieth century by the widespread ownership of cars, the construction of motorways and bridges, the use of high-speed trains, and by the development of fast, cheap air travel.

TRAVEL BY AIR

Fig. 5 shows the number of passengers starting or finishing journeys at Britain's airports from 1938 to 1987.

Fig. 5 *Air travellers to and from Britain (millions)*

	1938	1948	1968	1978	1987
World total	0.176	0.915	7.837	38.492	65.734
To/from Europe	—	—	6.190	27.883	48.193

- Draw a simple graph to show the information for 1968, '78 and '87.
- Why is it very difficult to show the figures for 1938 and '48 at the same scale on the same graph?
- Approximately what proportion of the total number of air travellers are on journeys to and from Europe?
  Remember, these figures are for all air travel, not just holidays.

Overseas visitors coming to Britain on holiday are only part of the air-travel picture. In 1980 17.5 million British people flew out of Britain through the main airports and by 1987 the number had reached nearly 27.5 million. Of these, nearly 20 million were travelling on holiday.

- When did the aeroplane become widely used by ordinary people for travelling abroad on holiday? Ask some older people about this. Did they ever fly when they were younger?

TRAVEL BY SEA

Although few people now make long journeys by sea, preferring the speed and convenience of the aeroplane, one kind of sea travel has continued to grow rapidly because it allows the growing number of car-owners access to other countries in Europe. This is the car ferry. Fig. 6 illustrates the growth in sea travel between 1968 and 1987. Note the high proportion travelling to continental Europe and Ireland—most of these will be passengers travelling in cars and coaches.

Fig. 6 *Passengers from Britain travelling by sea, 1968–1987 (millions)*

	1968	1978	1987
TOTAL PASSENGERS BY SEA	4.620	19.927	26.074
To/from Europe	3.554	17.400	23.327
To/from Ireland	0.870	2.316	2.581

- Draw simple graphs to illustrate these figures.
- For what reason might the pattern of car ferry travel be expected to change in the 1990s?

You will have seen from the information in the last few pages that holidays, and tourism and leisure activities generally, have increased considerably in quite a short time. Often it is hard to distinguish genuine tourist and leisure activities from other kinds of travel. For instance, if an overseas businessman visiting London decides to go to the theatre one evening and to spend a weekend relaxing in the country, is he on business or is he a tourist? In this example, his visit to Britain would not count as tourism but his leisure-time activities would. Remember that the figures you see have to try to take such complications into account. Some statistics divide tourists into categories such as 'holiday', 'visiting friends and relatives' (shortened to 'VFR'), 'business and conference' and a number of other categories. These categories can be quite important. For example, some resorts like Blackpool and Brighton are host to very large conferences and these bring extra visitors to the towns, often outside the peak holiday season. Conference delegates occupy hotels, eat meals in restaurants and visit local attractions during breaks in the conference proceedings.

ARE ALL HOLIDAYS THE SAME?

If there are different categories of tourists then there are certainly different kinds of holiday. We can put holidays into categories according to their duration (how long they are), the destination (seaside, mountains, cities, etc.), the type of accommodation used (hotel, camping, farmhouse, etc.) and the kind of organisation (package tour, individual, etc.).

Fig. 7 shows the types of accommodation used by British people on holiday both at home and abroad from 1951 to 1978.

- What changes have taken place in the kinds of accommodation used in Britain over this period?
- In what ways is the preferred accommodation different for holidays overseas?
- What kind of accommodation did your friends and relatives use on their last holiday? Do your results suggest that there may have been changes since 1978?

Figs. 7a & b Holiday accommodation used by British adults, 1951 to 1978
a) in Britain b) outside Britain
Source B.T.A. (British National Travel Survey)

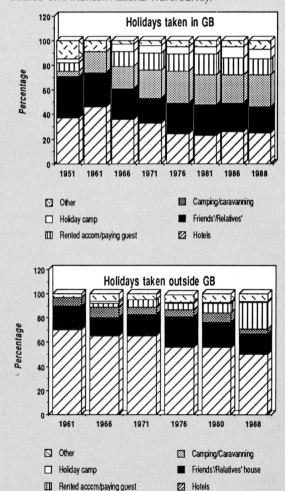

Tourism in Britain

WHERE DO VISITORS COME FROM?

Two kinds of people take holidays in Britain: British people visiting other parts of the country and people from overseas visiting Britain. The place where a tourist comes *from* is known as his/her 'origin'. The place he/she *visits* is called the 'destination'.

'HOME' VISITORS

The origin of home visitors is closely linked to Britain's population distribution. Those areas with high resident populations generate the largest numbers of visitors.

Fig. 8 shows the population distribution in the British Isles.

- Find, on the map, the following:
  London and the South East
  South-East Wales and Bristol
  Birmingham and the West Midlands
  Merseyside and Greater Manchester
  West Yorkshire
  The Tyne-Tees area
  Glasgow and Edinburgh.
- What do these areas have in common?

More evidence is available to show how unevenly Britain's population is spread. Consider these figures:

Region	Population
London and South East	16.7 millions
West Midlands	5.1 millions
North-West	6.4 millions

Britain's total population is about 54 millions.

- About what fraction of the entire population lives in the three regions listed above?

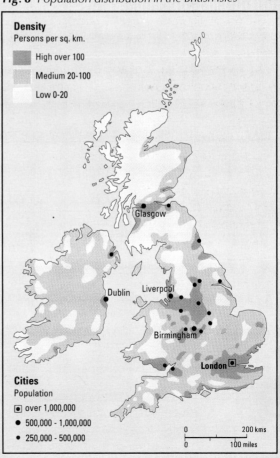

Fig. 8 *Population distribution in the British Isles*

Density
Persons per sq. km.

High over 100

Medium 20-100

Low 0-20

Glasgow

Dublin   Liverpool

Birmingham

London

Cities
Population
⊡ over 1,000,000
● 500,000 - 1,000,000
● 250,000 - 500,000

0   200 kms

0   100 miles

When you are studying such things as the location of Britain's holiday resorts or National Parks, keep in mind this information about Britain's population distribution. It is also an important factor in the location of the major airports.

In 1987 73 million holiday trips were made within Britain by British people. (A 'trip' means at least one night spent away from home.) These trips amounted to 340 million nights. (A 'night' is one night spent away from home by one person.) Two people on holiday for a fortnight would therefore count as two trips and 28 nights (2 × 14).

OVERSEAS VISITORS

Tourists visiting Britain from abroad account for a large slice of all tourism in Britain. Numbers are growing quickly. Here are some figures (millions):

Year	1973	1978	1983	1987
Trips	8.2	12.6	12.5	15.4
Nights	116	149	145	176

International holidays are affected by many factors—currency exchange rates, fears about security, etc. but despite some fluctuations the general trend is clearly upwards. As we shall see later, though, overseas visitors take different kinds of holidays from those preferred by home visitors.

- Draw separate pie charts for 'Trips' and 'Nights' to show the proportion of home to overseas visitors taking holidays in Britain in 1987.
- Explain the difference between the pie charts for 'Trips' and 'Nights'.

The origins of overseas visitors are as follows (1987 figures).

Country of Origin	Trips (000's)	Average duration (nights)	Spending (£ millions)
USA	2,800	10	1,480
France	2,000	9	370
West Germany	1,650	10	330
Irish Republic	1,030	8	290
Netherlands	860	6	160
Italy	680	14	270
Canada	590	14	230
Middle East	520	17	160
Australia	500	23	200
Belgium/Luxembourg	490	4	80
Other countries	4,300	11	2,630

The table also shows the number of nights' holiday, on average, spent in Britain and the total spending of people from each country on their British visits.

Now attempt the following tasks based on the information in the table.

- Rewrite the list in three sections headed 'Europe', 'North America' and 'Rest of World' (ignoring 'Other countries').
- Why do you think that most overseas visitors to Britain come from Europe?
- What reasons can you suggest for so many people from North America and Australia coming to Britain for holidays?
- Is there any connection between the distance travelled by overseas visitors and the number of nights they spend in Britain?

TOURIST DESTINATIONS IN BRITAIN

What kind of place comes to your mind when you think about tourists? Most people think of seaside resorts, famous buildings, old cities or special areas like National Parks. In fact, tourists can be found just about anywhere.

Britain has a rich and varied history and people have a wide variety of interests. Taking advantage of this, many towns and cities are attracting visitors by welcoming them to see old industrial sites or by arranging exhibitions about local history and industry. It is possible to visit a coal mine, go through a canal tunnel or see a nuclear power station. Every sporting interest is catered for and there are special interest holidays for photographers, walkers, bird-watchers, horse-riders, artists, anglers and every other hobby.

Sellafield Visitors' Centre

The tourist industry is therefore much more widespread than it used to be.

Figs. 9 and 10 overleaf show the distribution of British visitors in England and Wales and in Scotland.

Fig. 9 *Distribution of British visitors in Scotland, 1986 (by visitor nights)*

Source *S.T.B.*

Fig. 10 *Distribution of British visitors in England and Wales, 1986 (by visitor nights)*

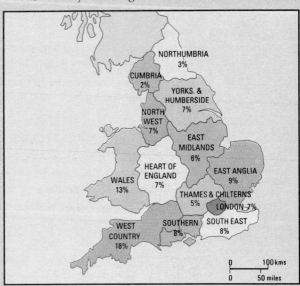

Source *British Tourism Survey*

● Make a list of the English and Welsh regions in order of importance for tourism.
● Do the same for the Scottish regions.
● Which English region attracted the largest percentage of visitors?
● How many tourist resorts and other attractions can you name in this region?
● Which region do you live in?
● Which other regions have you visited on holiday or for a day trip?
● Make a list—with brief details—of some tourist attractions near your home (perhaps in your county or city). Can you think of something in your area which might be of interest to visitors but which has not yet been developed as a tourist attraction?

WHERE DO VISITORS TO BRITAIN GO?

Many tourist attractions which appeal to British people are also visited by people on holiday in Britain from overseas.

● Use the figures given at the top of page 11 to make another map like Fig. 9, this time showing which parts of Britain were most frequently visited by *overseas* tourists (omitting 'Other').
● What are the main differences between the pattern shown for overseas visitors and that for British residents?
● Can you think of any reasons for these differences?

Region	% of Nights	Region	% of Nights
London	40.4	Yorks and Humberside	3.6
South East	9.2	Wales	2.6
Thames and Chilterns	6.7	East Midlands	2.5
West Country	6.0	Northumbria	1.7
North West	4.8	Cumbria	0.5
East Anglia	4.7		
Heart of England	4.7	Other	8.9
Southern	3.7		

PRINCIPAL DESTINATION AREAS IN BRITAIN

The following areas and towns are among the major holiday destinations for both British and overseas visitors in the British Isles:

Blackpool

Brighton

Channel Islands

Devon and Cornwall

Isle of Man

Isle of Skye

Isle of Wight

Norfolk Broads

Main historical and cultural centres include:

Bath

Cambridge

Dublin

Edinburgh

London

Stratford-on-Avon

Windsor

York

The Roman Baths and Bath Abbey

- Use an atlas to help you find each of these places, then mark them clearly on an outline map of the British Isles.
- Rewrite the list under the following headings:
  *SEASIDE RESORTS   ISLANDS   INLAND TOWNS AND CITIES
  OTHER AREAS*
- Each of the features in the list below is associated with one of the places in the lists on page 11. Match the features to the correct places.

TT motor cycle races	The National Railway Museum
Sailing and boating on rivers and dykes	The Roman Baths
	Dartmoor and Land's End
The Shakespeare Memorial Theatre	King's College Chapel
	The Needles

- Now try to connect these features with the correct places:
  Which two places have famous castles associated with the Royal family?
  Which two places have famous towers? In what ways are these towers very different from one another?
  Where will you find Sark and Alderney along with two better-known neighbours?
  Which place is not in Britain at all? In what country is it?
  Where could you see a Royal Pavilion, a large marina, two piers and still be only 50 miles from London?
- There were sixteen places and only fifteen features. The Isle of Skye is the missing place. Find it on an atlas map and then say what the following are: The Cuillins, Portree, Sound of Sleat.

NATIONAL PARKS

There are ten National Parks in England and Wales. Be very careful not to confuse them with other types of park, for example, Safari Parks, Amusement Parks or Theme Parks. National Parks are areas of outstandingly beautiful scenery often privately owned but under public management. Great care is taken to preserve the countryside for the enjoyment of everyone but many people still live and work there. There is no charge for visiting National Parks and no specially staged attractions. You can drive through or go walking, hill- or rock-climbing, camping, boating, horse-riding or take part in any outdoor activity you choose. The locations of the National Parks are shown in Fig. 11.

- Which National Park is nearest to where you live?
- Which main roads or motorways would you use to get to the Park?
- Try to find out something about the National Park nearest to you. What are its main attractions? What can you do there?
- Which National Parks are nearest to the following cities:
  Sheffield, Durham, Exeter?
- Which three National Parks are in Wales?
- Which National Park contains Windermere, Ullswater and Thirlmere?

INLAND WATERWAYS

Among the 'activity' holidays which have become very popular is cruising on canals and rivers in Britain. Holidaymakers can hire specially designed boats and spend a week or more navigating parts of the connected waterways system which, in earlier times, carried all kinds of cargo between inland towns and ports on the coast. Fig. 12 over the page shows the inland waterways of England and Wales. Using this map and using your own knowledge, try to answer the following questions:

Fig. 11 *The National Parks of England and Wales*

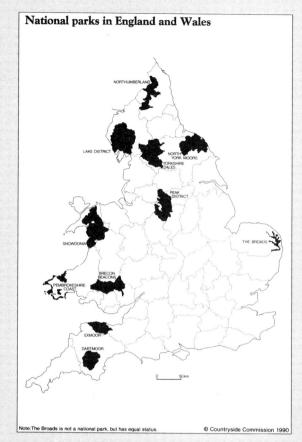

National parks in England and Wales

Note:The Broads is not a national park, but has equal status.   © Countryside Commission 1990

Source *Countryside Commission*

- Which canal connects London with Birmingham?
- Find a canal which crosses the border from England into Wales.
- Which waterways would allow you to travel right across England from Liverpool to The Wash?
- Which range of hills must be crossed by the Leeds and Liverpool Canal?
- How do waterways manage to climb over hills?
- Imagine you have been offered a two-week holiday on the waterways. You can start from anywhere you like but must return to your starting point at the end of your fortnight. Work out a suitable route allowing about 20 miles per day. List the waterways you will use and the principal places on the route. Try to give one piece of information about each place—perhaps brief details of tourist attractions in the area.

Different kinds of holidays appeal to different people.

- Describe the kinds of people who might enjoy a canal holiday.
- Are there some groups of people who would be less likely to go on the canals? Give the probable reasons.
- Collect information about other 'special interest' and 'activity' holidays.
- Ask your friends—including some adults—which of these special holidays they would enjoy and why they appeal to them.

Fig. 12 *Inland Waterways of England and Wales*

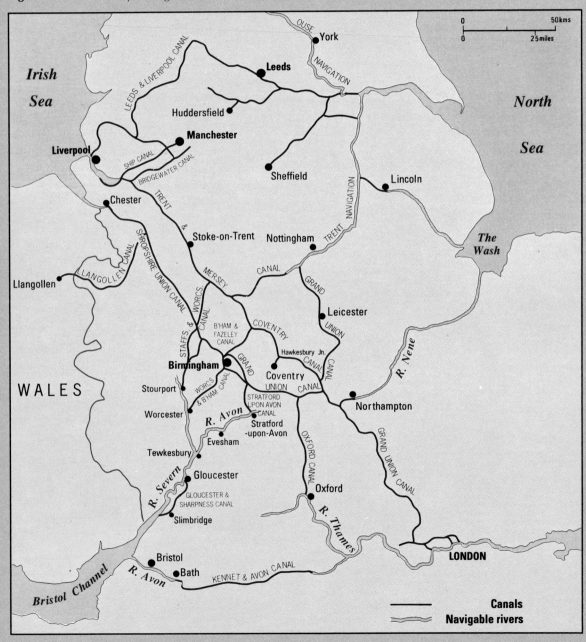

Holidays Abroad

While Britain itself attracts about 15 million visitors from overseas, many British people like to go abroad for their holidays.

- What reasons do people give for going on foreign holidays? Ask a variety of people and compile a list of reasons.

It is important to keep overseas holidays in perspective. About 80% of holidays by British people are taken in Britain leaving only about 20% going abroad. However, the overseas holidays tend to last longer and cost more so that the amount of money spent is divided as shown in Fig. 13.

Fig. 13 Spending on holidays at home and abroad

England
Wales/Scotland
Abroad

WHERE DO THEY GO?

There are holidays on offer all over the world. You can go to Iceland or the Amazon, on safari in East Africa or in the Australian Desert. You can cruise the Nile and see the pyramids or the canals of Venice and see the Rialto Bridge and St Mark's Church. If islands appeal to you there is a wide choice from the Canaries to the Falklands and from the Balearics to the West Indies.

- When you were reading the previous paragraph did you know immediately where all the places were? Use an atlas to help you find each place and then mark it on an outline map of the world.

While holidays to new and unusual destinations are becoming more popular, most people still head for a limited range of overseas destinations.

- Try to find ten or twenty people who have been on foreign holidays in the past few years and ask them where they went. Compare the results of your survey with the information given in Figs. 14 and 15 which show overseas holiday destinations in 1987.

Fig. 14 *UK visitors abroad—Principal destinations*

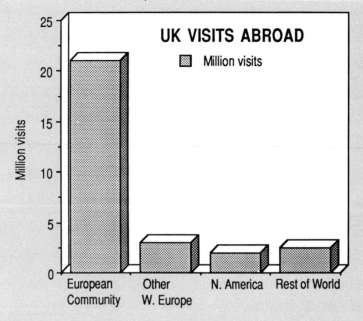

Year: 1987	Thousands of visits.
Spain	6,559
France	5,321
Greece	1,843
Irish Republic	1,528
West Germany	1,397
Italy	1,188
Netherlands	940
Portugal	903
Gibraltar/Malta/Cyprus	863
Rest of Europe	3,119

Fig. 15
UK holidays in Europe

You will see from the figures that by far the largest number of British people remain on the European continent for their holidays. Almost half of these holidays are taken in just two countries, Spain and France. There seems to be a fairly clear reason for the pattern shown: countries around the Mediterranean are very popular because of their climate and beaches while countries adjacent to Britain benefit from easy accessibility to British tourists.

Although much smaller than the European holiday business, leisure travel to the United States and Canada is nevertheless quite substantial. Relatively cheap trans-Atlantic air fares, the existence of many family ties between Britain and these countries and the range of tourist attractions available make them popular destinations.

EUROPEAN HOLIDAYS

You have seen already that, in Britain, there are many resorts and historical and cultural centres which attract visitors. Much the same factors apply in Europe. Here is a list of some popular holiday destinations in Europe.

Coastal Resorts:
>   Spain—The Balearics
>   The Canaries
>   Costa Blanca
>   Costa de Almeria
>   Costa Brava
>   Costa Del Sol
>   Costa Dorada.
> France/Italy/Yugoslavia—the Mediterranean and Adriatic coasts.
> Greece—Crete, Corfu and Rhodes.
> Portugal—The Algarve, Estoril.

Lakes, Mountains and Fjords:
>   The Alps—Switzerland and Austria.
>   Norway—the fjord coast.

The Spanish resort of Playa y Castillo

Although by no means an exhaustive list, anyone with an interest in the overseas tourist industry ought to know a little about these places—where they are, ways of getting to them and what they have to offer to British people on holiday. Fig. 16 shows Western Europe and identifies the places and areas in the above lists.

Fig. 16 *Western Europe—Principal holiday destinations*

Fig. 17 *Spain and Portugal showing main holiday areas*

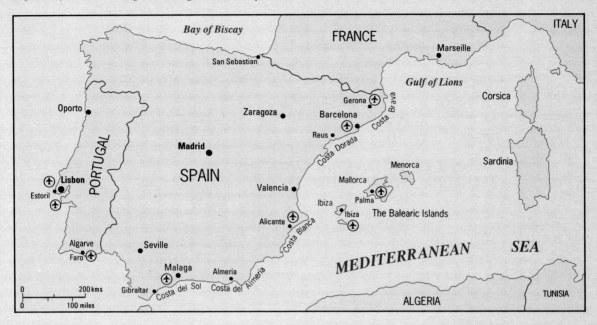

Fig. 18 *Greece and the Islands*

Figs. 17 and 18, on the previous page, are larger-scale maps of Spain and Portugal (known as the Iberian Peninsula) and Greece. Look carefully at these maps, compare them with atlas maps of the same areas and try to remember the names and locations.

● Make a list of the places shown in Figs. 17 and 18 according to the sea they are on, Atlantic, Mediterranean, or Adriatic. (Some countries have coasts on two seas.)

FINDING YOUR WAY AROUND THE MEDITERRANEAN RESORTS

● On a large sheet of paper, make a table to show some important details about each of the Mediterranean holiday regions. Your table could be set out like this:

Country	Holiday Region	Nearest Airport	Main Resorts
Spain	Costa Brava	Gerona/Barcelona	Lloret de Mar
			Tossa de Mar
			Estartit

Details for the Costa Brava have been given as an example. Extend your table by including these holiday regions:

COSTA DE ALMERIA, COSTA DORADA, COSTA BLANCA, COSTA DEL SOL, THE ALGARVE, ESTORIL, THE BALEARIC ISLANDS (Ibiza, Majorca, Minorca), CRETE, CORFU and RHODES.

Now add the following airports (sometimes, more than one airport is near to the holiday resorts):

REUS, PALMA, MALAGA, CHANIA, FARO, ALICANTE, IBIZA, CORFU, MINORCA, LISBON, RHODES, ALMERIA, HERAKLION.

Finally, sort out the following list of holiday resorts and complete your table:

PORTIMAO, ALMERIA, TORREMOLINOS, IPSOS, ARENAL D'EN CASTELL, KNOSSOS, PUERTO DE POLLENSA, SAN ANTONIO, CHANIA, MARBELLA, ROQUETAS DE MAR, RHODES, ALBUFEIRA, LINDOS, BENIDORM, PALMA NOVA, CASCAIS, ALICANTE.

Remember that there are numerous small resorts in all these areas and the selection above is only a small sample. One way to find out where the resorts are is to collect some holiday brochures. These often contain maps and short descriptions and photographs of the resorts.

OTHER MEDITERRANEAN HOLIDAY AREAS

France, Italy and Yugoslavia all have popular holiday resorts on their Mediterranean and Adriatic coasts. (Note that the Adriatic is part of the Mediterranean Sea.)

FRANCE   Although people often talk about 'the South of France' as a luxurious and romantic leisure area, comparatively few British people take holidays there. The resorts are, however, very popular with French people from the colder north of France. *CANNES, NICE, ST TROPEZ* and *ANTIBES* are among the better-known resorts here.

ITALY   Resorts in Italy are clustered in a few small groups. *LIDO DI JESOLO* is near Venice in the north-east, then, also on the Adriatic coast but further south are *RIMINI, RICCIONE, CATTOLICA* and *PESARO*. On the western side of the country, facing the Mediterranean are, in the north, *ALASSIO* and *DIANO MARINA*, further south, near Pisa with its famous leaning tower, are *VIAREGGIO* and the neighbouring *LIDO DI CAMAIOR* and finally, south of the Bay of Naples, are *SORRENTO, POSITANO* and *AMALFI*.

Italy has some very popular inland resorts, too. These are situated around some beautiful lakes in the north of the country. The lakes are *MAGGIORE, GARDA* and *COMO*. Although not offering the same attractions as the seaside resorts, the Alpine mountain scenery surrounding the lakes makes them a very attractive holiday setting.

YUGOSLAVIA   Almost the entire Yugoslavian coast is dotted with holiday resorts, some quite small. Among the better-known centres (from north to south) are *POREC, SPLIT* and *DUBROVNIK*. Unlike some of the other Mediterranean resorts, many of the Yugoslavian seaside towns are attractive old ports in their own right. This is true of Split and Dubrovnik.

● Use holiday brochures to find out which airports serve each of these holiday areas.

CULTURAL AND HISTORICAL CENTRES

Just as in Britain, many people are interested in the history, art and culture of other countries. For these people, visits to some of Europe's cities provide an enjoyable holiday or short break. Sometimes it is possible to spend a night or two in one of these centres during a journey by road or rail to more distant resorts.

Here is a list of some of the most important cities:

Amsterdam   Athens   Berlin   Brussels   Copenhagen   Florence
Madrid   Moscow   Munich   Paris   Prague   Rome   Salzburg   Vienna.

- Use your knowledge (or an atlas) to match each city with the country in which it is situated. Here are the countries—but not in the same order:

West Germany   France   Italy (2)   East Germany   Greece   Belgium
USSR   Netherlands   Austria (2)   Denmark   Czechoslovakia   Spain

- Take an outline map of Western Europe showing national boundaries and on it mark and name the cities and countries in your list. Mark the United Kingdom as well.
- Try to obtain some tourist information about each city, then write a brief summary of sights to be seen.

Copenhagen

THE RIVER RHINE

As well as being an important waterway for cargo vessels, the River Rhine is popular with tourists who can cruise all the way from the Netherlands to the Swiss border aboard luxury mini-liners which call at riverside towns in Germany and France *en route*.

- Add the River Rhine to your Western Europe map.
- From which mountains does the Rhine begin its journey?
- Into which sea does it eventually flow?

Rhine steamer passing St. Goarhausen

GETTING THERE

Journeys from Britain to the rest of Europe can be made in two ways: by surface transport (car, coach, train and ship) or by air. Since Britain is an island nation, all journeys involve a sea crossing (though the Channel Tunnel, when open, will make this factor less significant).

- Can you think of reasons why people might choose one form of transport rather than another for particular journeys?
  Here are some examples:
  Longer distances are covered much more quickly by air. Journeys to islands—such as the Balearics or the Canaries—are very difficult by surface transport, almost everyone goes there by air.
  People who live in southern England, close to the English Channel, can drive (using a car ferry) to France or Belgium more easily than those living in the north.
  Surface transport is slower but gives more opportunities to see the scenery along the route.
  Driving your own car allows you to carry more luggage—and gives you more freedom to travel around in your destination country.
  Going by train or coach avoids possible problems with driving on unfamiliar roads—and gives the driver a holiday, too!
- Ask some people who have taken holidays abroad how they travelled.

AIR AND SEA PORTS

Britain has many international airports and also sea ports providing drive-on/drive-off car ferry services. It is very difficult to separate the different reasons for peoples' journeys and so the passenger figures given in Figs. 19 and 20 are totals—including business and commercial travel as well as holiday and leisure travel. Nevertheless, they show the huge numbers of travellers being handled and give an indication of the relative importance of each port and airport.

Fig. 19 *Airport traffic in Britain, 1987*

Airport	Passengers (000)	% of UK total
London Heathrow	34,743	40.4
London Gatwick	19,381	22.5
Manchester	8,609	10.0
Glasgow	3,365	3.9
Birmingham	2,639	3.1
Luton	2,584	3.0
Belfast	2,116	2.5
Edinburgh	1,845	2.1
Aberdeen	1,469	1.7
Newcastle	1,335	1.6
East Midlands	1,287	1.5
Stansted (London)	713	0.8
Cardiff	652	0.7
Bristol	645	0.7
Leeds	625	0.7

Fig. 20 *Seaport traffic in Britain, 1987*

Car Ferry Port	Cars (000)	% of UK total
Dover (ship)	1,537	36.8
Dover (hovercraft)	238	5.7
Portsmouth	470	11.2
Harwich	242	5.8
Ramsgate	135	3.2
Hull	105	2.5
Sheerness	105	2.5
Newhaven	96	2.3
Felixstowe	84	2.0
Folkestone	80	1.9
All other UK ports (inc Scottish island ferries)	1,090	26.1

CHOOSING AN AIRPORT

One of the main advantages of flying is that it avoids the need for long overland journeys. Many people, therefore, like to start their overseas holiday by flying from an airport as near to their home as possible. For example, a family living in Bath would probably prefer to fly from Bristol Airport, less than 20 miles away, rather than having to drive or catch a train to one of the London airports.

● Select an airport from the list in Fig. 19 which would be convenient for people living in each of the following places:
    Stratford-on-Avon
    Brighton
    Blackpool
    The Scottish Highlands
    South Wales
    Northumberland

GETTING TO THE AIRPORT

Much of the benefit of flying is lost if it takes a long time to reach the departure airport. Motorways and railway stations adjacent to airports make such journeys much easier. Of the major international airports, only London (Gatwick) and Birmingham have main-line railway stations with direct access to the airport terminal buildings. A railway station will open at Stansted (with fast trains to London) in 1991 and there are plans for similar links to Manchester and to London (Heathrow) where the only rail connection is by the Piccadilly Line of London Underground.

Many airports have motorway access within a reasonable distance and some are immediately adjacent to a motorway.

● Which motorway would take passengers from London to Gatwick Airport?
● Luton airport lies just to the east of which motorway?
● Which motorways pass close to Bristol and Cardiff airports?
● Manchester and Leeds are each served by two major motorways. Which ones?
● How would you get from where you live to the nearest airports in the list in Fig. 19? Remember, holiday flights may not be available from your nearest airport so work out the best road route to two or three alternatives.
● How would you get to these airports by train or bus?

GETTING TO A FERRY PORT

Fig. 21 shows the main car ferry ports with services to the continent.

Fig. 21 *Main car ferry routes from Britain to the Continent*

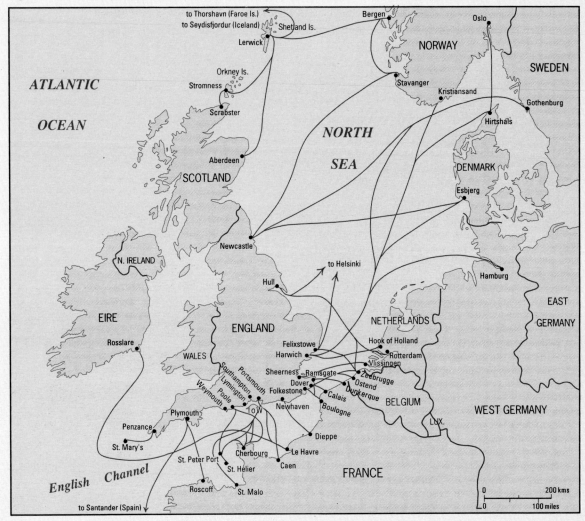

The ferry routes can be grouped broadly into three categories:

Group A: 'Short-Sea' ports with services to France and Belgium across the narrowest part of the English Channel. Crossings take from $1\frac{1}{2}$ to $3\frac{1}{2}$ hours.

Group B: Other Channel ports with services to France and Spain over longer routes. These take between 4 and 24 hours.

Group C: North Sea ports. From these ports there are ferries to the Netherlands, Belgium and West Germany and to Scandinavian countries—Denmark, Norway and Sweden. Most of these crossings are also long.

Holiday motorists would probably choose their car-ferry port according to which country they planned to visit and the most convenient route from their home town.

Ferry operators often change ports to meet changing demands. The ferry routes and the ports they serve as shown in Fig. 21 were the ones being operated in 1989 but it is always best to check from the firms' brochures which routes they are currently operating.

- Suggest a suitable ferry route for each of the following motorists:

HOME TOWN	DESTINATION COUNTRY
Birmingham	Netherlands
Bristol	Spain
Southampton	Norway
London	France (north east)
Cambridge	France (west)
Liverpool	Belgium

- Now use your own knowledge and (if necessary) a road atlas to find suitable routes (on motorways wherever possible) to get these motorists from their homes to their ferry ports.
- Would it be best to change any of your recommended ferry ports now that you have checked on suitable road routes? The nearest port is not always the easiest to get to.

JOURNEY TIMES

People travelling abroad—by sea or by air—must allow for a number of factors which may extend their journey times quite considerably. Here are some points to bear in mind:

1 Extra time must be allowed to get to the airport or seaport. This is to allow for breakdowns, traffic problems or even getting lost in an unfamiliar area. Planes and ships will not wait for latecomers and a missed departure could ruin the holiday.

2 Check-in time. Most airlines and car-ferry operators require passengers to present themselves for ticket and other checks at least one hour and sometimes two or three hours before scheduled departure time.

Checking-in at Heathrow Airport
© *Heathrow Airport 1990*

3   Time-zone changes. Most journeys abroad take travellers across time zones. Places east of Britain (Europe, for example) are ahead of British time, places to the west (the USA, for example) are behind. Large countries like the USA themselves spread over several time zones. Travellers must add or take away the correct number of hours from apparent journey times.

Here is an example:

> France is, for most of the year, one hour ahead of Britain. A Channel crossing taking six hours would leave the English port at 06.00 and reach the French port at 13.00 (*not* 12.00 as you might expect). On the return crossing the ship would leave France at 12.00, take six hours on the crossing and reach the English port at 17.00.

It is very important to check all departure and arrival times carefully to make sure that you have allowed for these time changes where necessary. With air travel over short distances (London to Amsterdam, for example) the outward flight can appear to take two hours in the timetable while the return trip seems to touch down in London at the same moment that it takes off from Amsterdam!

4   Arrival at the foreign air or seaport usually involves a considerable amount of time to get off the plane or ship, to get to and through the terminal buildings, to pass through customs and passport checks and to find the way out of the port or airport and towards the final destination.

All these additional time factors can add up to a very much longer overall journey time. Where public transport is involved—train or bus, for example—plenty of time needs to be allowed for making connections and changing. In some cities it is necessary to go across the city centre to get from one station to another when changing trains. In a city you do not know well this can take a long time and carrying luggage is often an added problem.

Remember all these points when planning a journey.

World Travel

Holidays to more distant parts of the world are becoming steadily more popular. Few people can claim to know every part of the world in great detail but it is important, especially for anyone working in the tourism and travel industry, to have a sound general knowledge of the world's continents, major regions and oceans.

Many descriptions are in common use to identify different parts of the world. Make sure you understand what they mean.

NORTH, SOUTH, EAST AND WEST

These are more than just compass directions.
For example:

The Southern Hemisphere—is everywhere south of the Equator.
The Northern Hemisphere—is everywhere north of the Equator.
'The West' has no precise meaning, but is often used to refer to North America, Europe and, sometimes, other developed parts of the world.
South Africa is a country; *southern* Africa refers to the southern half of the *continent* of Africa.
South America is a continent (containing many countries, such as Chile and Brazil) but in the USA (United States of America) 'The South' means the southern states such as Tennessee and Alabama.

Try to find other examples of special meanings for compass directions.

* What are the 'Middle East' and 'Far East'?
* Where is New South Wales?
* In Ireland, what is meant by 'The North' and 'The South'?

OCEANS AND CONTINENTS

Can you distinguish between a continent and a country, a sea and an ocean?
* Find the odd one out in each of the following lists:
  1 Africa, Antarctica, Australasia, Arctica, Europe.
  2 Indian, Pacific, Mediterranean, Southern, Arctic.
  3 United States, South America, Africa, Europe, Asia.
* Name two other countries, besides India, which make up the Indian sub-continent.
* To which continent does Japan belong?
* Which ocean separates North America from Asia?

- Which two continents lie on either side of the South Atlantic?
- Only two continents are entirely in the Southern Hemisphere. Which are they?
- When people in Britain say they are going 'to the continent', which continent do they mean?
- People in the USA say that their country stretches 'from sea to shining sea'. Which seas (or, rather, oceans) are they talking about?

MOUNTAINS AND RIVERS

Many ranges of mountains and major rivers have special importance for world travellers. Sometimes they mark the boundary between countries, sometimes they are tourist attractions in themselves, sometimes they are used to describe a region.

The Canadian Rocky Mountains

● Connect each river or mountain range on the left with a feature from the list on the right:

Amazon	The Pyramids
Himalayas	Lake Titicaca
The Rockies	Rain forests
The Alps	Mount Everest
The Nile	Mont Blanc
The Andes	Canadian Pacific Railway

● When you think you are sure you know the oceans, continents and major rivers and mountains, try marking them on a world outline map. Check with the atlas.

CITIES

● Arrange the following cities into two lists—those north and those south of the Equator.

London	New York	Rio de Janeiro	Hong Kong
Sydney	Beijing (Peking)	Rotterdam	Singapore.

● Which cities would you say were definitely 'western' cities, which are 'in the far-east' and which do not fit either category?
● Suggest something a tourist might like to see or do in each of these cities.

Hong Kong

London

OTHER WORLD FEATURES

- Do you know at which pole you would find the Arctic and which the Antarctic?
- You could sail on a cruise ship along the coastline of which European country and pass inside the Arctic Circle?
- Why could such a cruise be advertised as 'Journey to the Midnight Sun'? Would this description be accurate right through the year?
- Find, in an atlas, the Tropic of Cancer and the Tropic of Capricorn. Which one is north of the Equator and which is south?

The area around and between these lines is often referred to as 'The Tropics'.

- Which of the cities listed on page 31 could be described as being 'in The Tropics'?
- What features of 'The Tropics' might make it an area where tourists would need to take special precautions?
- Find out how tropical climates differ from those in Mediterranean resorts.
- Which desert lies between the Mediterranean and 'The Tropics'?

FLYING AROUND THE WORLD

Unlike ships, aeroplanes can follow more or less direct routes over land or sea. Nevertheless, planes on very long flights, from Britain to Australia or Japan, for example, must make refuelling stops. These stops are frequently used by tourists as 'stopovers': they break their journey for 24 or 48 hours and take the opportunity to see the local sights.

Fig. 22, on the following page, shows some of the major world air routes.

- Suggest likely stopover cities on the following routes:
    London—Sydney (Australia)
    London—Tokyo (Japan)
    London—San Francisco (USA)
    New York—Delhi (India)
    Rio de Janeiro—Beijing/Peking (China)

Heathrow Airport
© *Heathrow Airport 1990*

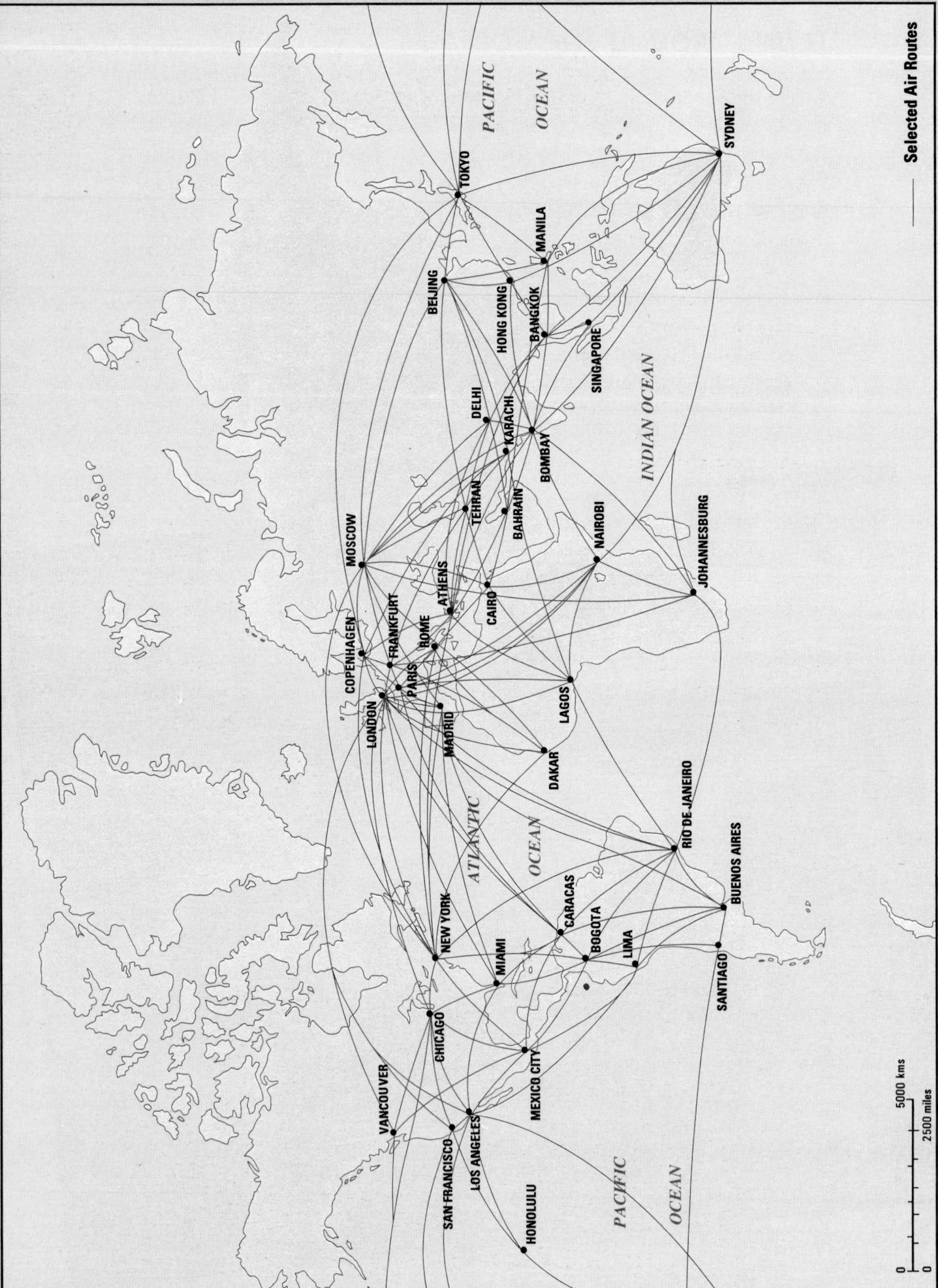

Fig. 22 Principal World Air Routes

Selected Air Routes

PACIFIC OCEAN

SYDNEY

TOKYO

MANILA

BEIJING

HONG KONG

BANGKOK

SINGAPORE

INDIAN OCEAN

DELHI

KARACHI

BOMBAY

TEHRAN

BAHRAIN

NAIROBI

MOSCOW

ATHENS

CAIRO

JOHANNESBURG

COPENHAGEN

FRANKFURT

ROME

PARIS

LONDON

MADRID

LAGOS

DAKAR

RIO DE JANEIRO

ATLANTIC OCEAN

BUENOS AIRES

NEW YORK

CARACAS

MIAMI

BOGOTA

LIMA

CHICAGO

SANTIAGO

VANCOUVER

MEXICO CITY

SAN FRANCISCO

LOS ANGELES

HONOLULU

PACIFIC OCEAN

5000 kms

2500 miles

0

0

Planning Holidays

You will remember from Chapter 1 that a holiday is often the most expensive item people buy other than their house and car. It is not surprising that much care and time often goes into planning a holiday. Travel agencies and tourist information offices employ specialists to offer help and advice to people planning their holidays. Perhaps you are considering such a career yourself. Almost everyone, at some time, needs to be able to plan a journey or a longer holiday. To do this properly you need two things: information and the skill to use it fully.

INFORMATION

There has never been so much information available as there is today. Most of it is contained in books, brochures, maps and leaflets available from libraries, book shops, travel agents, tourist information offices and from individual tourist attractions. Computer technology provides still more information for anyone with a terminal through services such as *Prestel* while everyone has access to television and radio programmes which are a further source of information on many aspects of travel and tourism.

Start collecting as much information as you can relating to tourism and leisure. You should not need to buy very much, if anything. Most items are readily available free of charge. Here are some suggestions:

1 Package holiday brochures (from holiday companies or agents).
2 Car ferry brochures (from ferry companies or agents).
3 Airline schedules (from airlines or agents).
4 Coach, bus and railway timetables. Local ones are often free but larger timetable books can be expensive. However, last year's should be available and for practice purposes would be good enough.
5 Resort brochures (from the publicity office of each resort).
6 Hotel locations, facilities and prices (from major hotel chains).
7 Leaflets about individual tourist attractions (from the attractions themselves or from tourist information offices).
8 Maps—town plans, road, railway, airline, etc. Often included in brochures and timetables. Some are free from tourist offices.

Try writing a polite letter to a local travel agent asking if you could collect any out-of-date brochures from time to time. This is better than taking current ones from the display when genuine holiday customers may need them. Some travel agents are even kind enough to pass on old timetables and other reference books to be used for practice purposes.

USING INFORMATION PROPERLY

Possessing information is only a start; learning to use it properly is very important. Many of the skills you will need will have been gained from work in geography and other lessons in school or college. Remember, though, that you will often need to combine pieces of information, compare one item with another and use common sense to find solutions to problems. You must not expect there to be only one right answer if only you can find the correct page in the book! Often there is a bewildering selection of alternatives and trying to find the good and bad points about each one is rather like the work of a detective.

   Some of the specific skills you will need include:
1 Reading all kinds of maps—road atlases, diagrams of railway, underground, airline or bus routes, weather and climate maps, street and building plans, even deck plans of cruise ships.
2 Using timetables—these are set out in many different ways but always you need to be sure you are looking at travel in the right direction, on the right day and that any connections allow enough time.
3 Reading diagrams and charts—prices of rooms, car ferry rates, climate statistics, etc.

4 Understanding the needs of the people for whom the holiday or journey is being planned. You must make sure that you have asked all the right questions and noted the answers so that you can work out suitable routes, types of transport or accommodation and suggest appropriate places to visit and things to see.

There are some examples of information here and on pages 38 to 40. Make sure you know how to use this material by answering the questions which follow.

Olau Line car ferry tariffs

55 + Special

Save up to £70

A special return fare for those aged 55 and over. Available on day sailings only throughout the year (1 Jan – 31 Dec), provided both passengers are aged 55 and over, and that the car conforms to Vehicle category 1 (see Vehicle Tariff opposite).

Two adults and car (return on any **day** sailing).

The cost is **£88** return.

up to 53 hours on the continent

53 Hour Return

Up to 53 hours on the Continent available on all sailings throughout the year.

The cost is **£25** return fare for each adult.

and **£15** return fare for each child (4 – 13 years).

infants under 4 years of age travel **FREE**

Cars or other vehicle (conforming to category 1, see Vehicle Tariff opposite) **50% discount** of the applicable rate for each sailing. This is not applicable to vehicle categories 2-6 (see Vehicle Tariffs opposite), or valid with vehicles towing trailers/caravans etc).

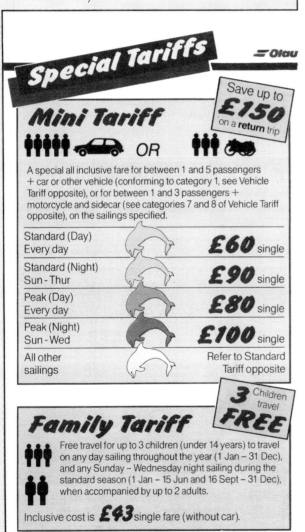

Special Tariffs — Olau

Mini Tariff

Save up to £150 on a return trip

OR

A special all inclusive fare for between 1 and 5 passengers + car or other vehicle (conforming to category 1, see Vehicle Tariff opposite), or for between 1 and 3 passengers + motorcycle and sidecar (see categories 7 and 8 of Vehicle Tariff opposite), on the sailings specified.

Standard (Day) Every day	**£60** single
Standard (Night) Sun - Thur	**£90** single
Peak (Day) Every day	**£80** single
Peak (Night) Sun - Wed	**£100** single
All other sailings	Refer to Standard Tariff opposite

3 Children travel FREE

Family Tariff

Free travel for up to 3 children (under 14 years) to travel on any day sailing throughout the year (1 Jan – 31 Dec), and any Sunday – Wednesday night sailing during the standard season (1 Jan – 15 Jun and 16 Sept – 31 Dec), when accompanied by up to 2 adults.

Inclusive cost is **£43** single fare (without car).

Accommodation Tariffs	single journey (£'s)		Sailings	
			Day	Night
Luxury outside cabin	One double bed and two single berths, shower/toilet	Per cabin	35.00	58.00
2-berth outside cabin	Shower/toilet	Per berth	8.50	14.00
2-berth inside cabin	Shower/toilet	Per berth	8.00	13.00
4-berth inside cabin	Shower/toilet	Per berth	5.00	8.50
4-berth inside couchette	(Olau Hollandia)	Per berth	2.50	4.00
3-berth inside couchette	(Olau Britannia)	Per berth	2.50	4.00
Pullman seat		Per seat	*FREE*	2.50

Note: Cabin categories and prices for accommodation on the new Olau vessel (to be introduced late 1989) are detailed on page 29.

Gold Star Holidays to London

Rail Inclusive Breaks / Freedom BREAKS

Prices per person for 1 night* 3 April '89 to 31 October '89 inclusive – (Note supplements June to October inc.) including accommodation, full breakfast, Visitor Travelcard and rail travel from stations in:

Avon D	Dorset C	Hants B	Mid Glamorgan D	Staffs C
Beds A	Dumfries F	Hereford & Worcs C	Norfolk C	Strathclyde G
Berks A	Durham F	Herts A	N Yorks E	Suffolk B
Bucks A	Dyfed E	Highland H	Northants B	Surrey A
Cambs B	E Sussex A	Humberside E	Northumberland F	Tayside H
Cent Scotland G	Essex A	IOW C	Notts D	Tyne & Wear B
Cheshire D	Fife G	Kent A	Oxon B	Warwicks B
Cleveland F	Gloucs C	Lancs E	Powys D	W Glamorgan D
Clwyd D	Grampian H	Leics C	Shrops C	W Midlands B
Cornwall E	Gtr London A	Lincs D	Somerset D	W Sussex A
Cumbria E	Gtr Manchester D	Lothian G	S Glamorgan D	W Yorks E
Derbys D	Gwent D	Merseyside D	S Yorks D	Gwynedd E
Devon E	Gwynedd E			

Freedom BREAKS — Prices per person from 3 April '89 to 31 October '89 inclusive – (Note supplements June to October inc.) including accommodation, full breakfast and Visitor Travelcard.

Hotel No.	LONDON HOTELS (Loc: LO)	A £	B £	C £	D £	E £	F £	G £	H £	Add for EACH EXTRA NIGHT £	Add for ALL NIGHTS June to October inc. £	for 1 night* £	Add for EACH EXTRA NIGHT £	Seasonal Supps. Add for ALL NIGHTS June to Oct. inc. £
1040	Forum	53	59	62	67	71	85	94	100	39.50	5.50	44	39.50	5.50
1042	Grosvenor ■	53	59	62	67	71	85	94	100	39.50	2.50	44	39.50	2.50
1044	London Tara	52	58	61	66	70	84	93	99	38.50	4.50	43	38.50	4.50
1046	Onslow	51	57	60	65	69	83	92	98	38.00	n.c.	42	38.00	n.c.
1048	Hospitality Inn Piccadilly	51	57	60	65	69	83	92	98	37.50	4.00	42	37.50	4.00
1050	Charing Cross ■	51	57	60	65	69	83	92	98	37.50	2.50	42	37.50	2.50
1052	Ibis Euston ■	51	57	60	65	69	83	92	98	37.50	n.c.	42	37.50	n.c.
1054	Kensington Park	50	56	59	64	68	82	91	97	36.50	6.00	41	36.50	6.00
1056	Regency	50	56	59	64	68	82	91	97	36.50	4.00	41	36.50	4.00
1058 1060 1062 1064	Green Park Londoner Rembrandt Rubens	50	56	59	64	68	82	91	97	36.50	1.50	41	36.50	1.50
1066	Bedford Corner ■	49	55	58	63	67	81	90	96	36.00	5.50	40	36.00	5.50
	InterCity 1st class Travel Supplement	3	6	8	10	13	19	23	27	n.c.= No additional charge				

* 1 night breaks available Fri/Sat/Sun nights only. 2 or more night breaks available any night   ■ = Mid-week breaks available

Caledonian MacBrayne Ferry Timetable

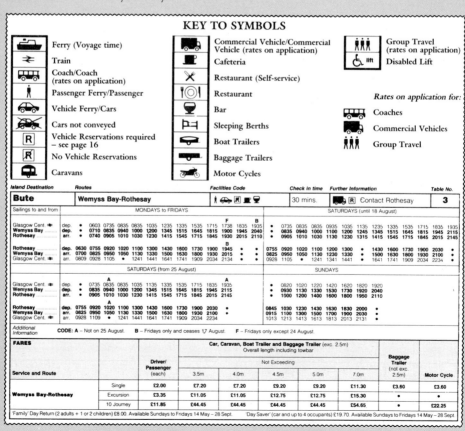

KEY TO SYMBOLS

- Ferry (Voyage time)
- Train
- Coach/Coach (rates on application)
- Passenger Ferry/Passenger
- Vehicle Ferry/Cars
- Cars not conveyed
- R Vehicle Reservations required – see page 16
- R̸ No Vehicle Reservations
- Caravans
- Commercial Vehicle/Commercial Vehicle (rates on application)
- Cafeteria
- Restaurant (Self-service)
- Restaurant
- Bar
- Sleeping Berths
- Boat Trailers
- Baggage Trailers
- Motor Cycles
- Group Travel (rates on application)
- lift Disabled Lift

Rates on application for:
- Coaches
- Commercial Vehicles
- Group Travel

Island Destination	Routes	Facilities Code	Check in time	Further Information	Table No.
Bute	**Wemyss Bay–Rothesay**	🚶🚗 R ☕ 🍷	30 mins.	R Contact Rothesay	**3**

Sailings to and from

MONDAYS to FRIDAYS

												F		B
Glasgow Cent. ⇌	dep.	●	0603	0735	0835	0835	1035	1235	1335	1535	1715	1738	1835	1935
Wemyss Bay	dep.	●	0710	0835	0940	1000	1200	1345	1515	1645	1815	1900	1945	2040
Rothesay	arr.	●	0740	0905	1010	1030	1230	1415	1545	1715	1845	1930	2015	2110

											B		
Rothesay	dep.	0630	0755	0920	1020	1100	1300	1430	1600	1730	1900	1945	●
Wemyss Bay	arr.	0700	0825	0950	1050	1130	1330	1500	1630	1800	1930	2015	●
Glasgow Cent. ⇌	arr.	0809	0928	1105	●	1241	1441	1641	1741	1909	2034	2134	

SATURDAYS (until 18 August)

	●	0735	0835	0835	0935	1035	1135	1235	1335	1535	1715	1835	1935
	●	0835	0940	1000	1100	1200	1245	1345	1515	1645	1815	1945	2115
	●	0905	1010	1030	1130	1230	1315	1415	1545	1715	1845	2015	2145

	0755	0920	1020	1100	1200	1300	●	1430	1600	1730	1900	2030
	0825	0950	1050	1130	1230	1330	●	1500	1630	1800	1930	2100
	0928	1105	●	1241	1341	1441		1641	1741	1909	2034	2234

SATURDAYS (from 25 August)

			A								A		
Glasgow Cent. ⇌	dep.	0735	0835	0835	1035	1135	1335	1535	1715	1835	1935
Wemyss Bay	dep.	0835	0940	1000	1200	1345	1515	1815	1945	2115
Rothesay	arr.	0905	1010	1030	1230	1415	1545	1715	1845	2015	2145

SUNDAYS

	●	0820	1020	1220	1420	1620	1820	1920
	●	0930	1130	1330	1530	1730	1920	2040
	●	1000	1200	1400	1600	1800	1950	2110

			A								
Rothesay	dep.	0755	0920	1020	1100	1300	1430	1600	1730	1900	2030	●
Wemyss Bay	arr.	0825	0950	1050	1130	1330	1500	1630	1800	1930	2100	●
Glasgow Cent. ⇌	arr.	0928	1109	●	1241	1441	1641	1741	1909	2034	2234	

	0845	1030	1230	1430	1630	1830	2000	●
	0915	1100	1300	1500	1700	1900	2030	●
	1013	1213	1413	1613	1813	2013	2131	●

Additional Information **CODE: A** – Not on 25 August.   **B** – Fridays only and ceases 17 August.   **F** – Fridays only except 24 August.

FARES

Car, Caravan, Boat Trailer and Baggage Trailer (exc. 2.5m) Overall length including towbar

Service and Route		Driver/ Passenger (each)	Not Exceeding					Baggage Trailer (not exc. 2.5m)	Motor Cycle
			3.5m	4.0m	4.5m	5.0m	7.0m		
	Single	£2.00	£7.20	£7.20	£9.20	£9.20	£11.30	£3.60	£3.60
Wemyss Bay–Rothesay	Excursion	£3.35	£11.05	£11.05	£12.75	£12.75	£15.30	●	●
	10 Journey	£11.85	£44.45	£44.45	£44.45	£44.45	£54.65	●	£22.25

'Family' Day Return (2 adults + 1 or 2 children) £8.00. Available Sundays to Fridays 14 May – 28 Sept.   'Day Saver' (car and up to 4 occupants) £19.70. Available Sundays to Fridays 14 May – 28 Sept.

Typical Car Hire Charges at Continental Airports

FLY CAR

PRE-BOOKED CAR HIRE PRICE (£)

Airport	7 night holiday (7 x 24hr days rental)* CAR GROUP					Each additional night (additional 24hrs of rental)* CAR GROUP				
	1	2	3	4	5	1	2	3	4	5
Salzburg, Klagenfurt Innsbruck, Vienna	98	112	147	203	161	14	16	21	29	23
Geneva (for Swiss resorts), Zurich, Berne	105	119	133	140	161	15	17	19	20	23
Geneva (for French resorts)	119	147	168	231	217	17	21	24	33	31
Milan	119	133	140	189	259	17	19	20	27	37
Bergen	154	175	203	238	-	22	25	29	34	-

* Note: Rates apply to 24 hour days from the time of hire. Any extra part day is charged locally at the full additional daily rate.

Airport	Examples of extras payable locally in local currency on returning car		
	CDW (optional but recommended)	Personal Accident Insurance (optional)	Local Tax (compulsory)
Salzburg, Klagenfurt Innsbruck, Vienna	AS 140 Per day	AS 50 Per day	
Geneva (for Swiss resorts), Zurich, Berne	SFr 14-19 Per day†	SFr 10 Per day	21.2%
Geneva (for French resorts)	FFr 48 to 63 Per day†	FFr 21 Per day	No Tax
Milan	L.10,000-13,600 Per day†	L.5,500 Per day	33.3%
Bergen	NKr 45-50 Per day†	NKr 20 Per day	22%
			20%

† Varies according to group of car

Airport	CAR GROUP - Make or model available (or similar)				
	1	2	3	4	5
Salzburg, Klagenfurt Innsbruck, Vienna	Fiat Panda	Ford Fiesta	Ford Escort	Ford Sierra	Ford Escort Automatic
Geneva (for Swiss resorts), Zurich, Berne	Fiat Panda	Ford Fiesta	Ford Escort	Ford Orion	Ford Sierra Automatic
Geneva (for French resorts)	Ford Fiesta	Peugeot 205	Ford Escort	Ford Sierra	Opel Ascona Automatic
Milan	Fiat Panda	Fiat Uno	Ford Escort	Fiat Regata	Opel Ascona Automatic
Bergen	Ford Fiesta	VW Golf	Ford Sierra	Volvo 240	-

HOW TO BOOK

Just tick the relevant box on the booking form and we will send you further details and an application form which you should complete and return.
* Car hire applications must be received not later than 14 days prior to departure.
* Drivers must be over 23 years old and hold a full British driving licence.

Martin Rooks Holidays Flight Information—Costa del Sol

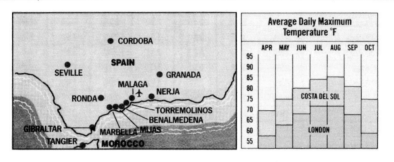

FLIGHT INFORMATION Most holidays on these pages are available on the flights shown below. Any supplements indicated should be added to the basic holiday price.

DEPARTURES TO MALAGA

Departure Airport	Holiday Nights	Departure Day/Time	Return Day/Time	First Dep	Last Dep	Flight Supp
GATWICK	7, 14	Sun 1645	Sun 2300	16 Apr	22 Oct	Nil
LUTON	7, 14	Sun 1420	Sun 2045	07 May	22 Oct	Nil
BOURNEMOUTH	7, 14	Wed 1530	Wed 1430	03 May	18 Oct	Nil
BIRMINGHAM	7, 14	Wed 0800	Wed 2200	16 Apr	18 Oct	Nil
MANCHESTER	7, 14	Sun 0800	Sun 1500	16 Apr	22 Oct	£15
GLASGOW	7, 14	Sun 0845	Sun 1615	07 May	22 Oct	£30*

The last 14 night departures are one week earlier than the dates shown.
All timings are approximate and subject to final confirmation.

*Add £20 30 May – 19 July
05 Oct – 18 Oct

QUESTIONS

1 How many passengers can sail on the Olau Line 'Mini Tariff' with a car? How much will a return trip cost them on Tuesday night crossing in the peak period?

2 Mr Dutch is 56 and his wife is 54. Can they use the Olau '55 + Special' fare?
How much would they have saved compared with the 'Mini Tariff'? (They planned to travel both ways on a day sailing in the Standard period.)

3 Mr and Mrs Dutch decide to have a cabin so that they can relax during the crossing. How much will a two-berth cabin cost them? What do you think is meant by 'outside' and 'inside'?

4 Mr Scott, who lives on the Isle of Bute in the Clyde estuary, is planning a weekend break in London. The price of the rail-inclusive break depends on the length of journey and the hotel chosen.
In which lettered zone is Strathclyde where Mr Scott lives?

5 How much will a one-night visit to the Grosvenor Hotel cost?

6   What will be included in this price in addition to rail fares and the hotel room?

7   If he decides to stay an extra night, how much more will he have to pay?

8   Work out Mr Scott's total bill for two nights at the Grosvenor with first-class rail travel from Strathclyde in August.

9   Mr Scott wants to get from his home at Rothesay, Isle of Bute, to Glasgow as early as possible on the Saturday morning to catch his train to London. When does the first ferry leave Rothesay on Saturdays?

10   How long does the crossing to Wemyss Bay take?

11   At what time will Mr Scott get to Glasgow?

12   At which Glasgow station will he arrive?

13   On his return from London on Monday, at what time does the last ferry leave Wemyss Bay?

14   At what time does the connecting train leave Glasgow?

15   What other information about the Rothesay–Wemyss Bay ferry can you find out from the timetable?

16   Ina Sunspot from Liverpool has enquired about a fortnight's holiday on the Costa Del Sol. Find the following information for her from the tour operator's brochure:

       The nearest airport to Ina's home.

       The day and time of the flight from that airport.

       The cost of any supplements, etc. (The holiday is in August.)

       The name of the airport she will fly to in Spain.

       The names of some coastal resorts in the area.

       The average daily maximum temperature she can expect on the Costa Del Sol.

       The day and time of her arrival back in Britain.

17   After all your hard work, Miss Sunspot says she would prefer to travel midweek. What alternative airport would you recommend and what changes are now needed to the information you have just been working out?

18   To make the most of their holiday in Switzerland, the Yodel family plan to hire a car from Zurich Airport. They need the car from 13.00 on Sunday, May 12th until 21.00 on Sunday, May 19th. What will be the hire charge for a Group 4 car?

19   What kind of car will they be getting?

20   How much extra will personal accident insurance cost them per day? What currency will they have to use to pay for it?

Notice the variety of different ways in which all this information has been presented. It would be surprising if you looked up everything correctly at the first attempt—yet people who work in the travel business must ensure that they do not overlook any details or make mistakes because very serious problems could result.

You need to take special care about:

All footnotes and 'small print'—these often contain restrictions or details of extra charges.

Whether fares are return fares or one-way only.

Special prices or special offers—usually there are restrictions on who can use them and when.

'Days' and 'nights'—a three-day holiday includes two nights and a week (say Saturday to Saturday) is eight days.

These are points to which you need to pay particular attention if you decide to work in the industry.

Using Skills and Knowledge

As with most things, the more you use and practise the skills needed for travel and tourism the more knowledgeable and efficient you will become. There are three important areas at which you need to work and gain experience:

1 KNOWLEDGE—there are no short cuts here; your basic geographical knowledge is very important. It enables you to visualise journeys and places, to anticipate climatic conditions, to know where to look in atlases, guide books, etc. and (very important) to give other people the impression that you know what you are doing.

2 SKILLS—selecting the right maps, charts, timetables, etc. reading them correctly, remembering to allow for time differences, walking between stations, being delayed, etc. comparing prices and other details of hotels, flights, entertainments, etc.

3 DECISION-MAKING—taking into account all the information you can collect, making decisions that are sensible and fit all the circumstances well. This includes understanding the needs of different people—the young or old, active or lazy, the disabled. Remember, good decisions depend on adequate knowledge and skills.

As you work through the questions in this chapter, ask yourself which of these three areas you are practising and make your own assessment of how good you are at each. Answers to some of the questions—together with hints about how you should have tackled them—are given in a separate section at the end of this chapter.

Draw a chart like the one below and tick the boxes to show how you are improving.

Self Assessment Chart	Good	Average	Poor
Knowledge			
Skills			
Decision-making			

HOLIDAYS IN BRITAIN

Fig. 23 *UK Tourist Board Regions*

1 a You are starting work in a travel agent's office and have been asked to file some new British Isles holiday brochures in the correct part of the filing cabinet. The sections are labelled according to the Tourist Boards' regions. These are shown in Fig. 23. Here are the titles of the brochures:

THE ENGLISH LAKES
THE ISLE OF WIGHT
ANTRIM AND GIANT'S CAUSEWAY
THE EDINBURGH FESTIVAL
SHAKESPEARE COUNTRY
BOATING ON THE BROADS
CANTERBURY AND THE CINQUE PORTS
WEEKENDS IN OXFORD
CLIMBING IN THE CAIRNGORMS
SPECTACULAR SKYE
HEATHROW HOTELS
LINCOLNSHIRE BULBFIELDS COACH TOUR
TORQUAY: THE ENGLISH RIVIERA

Say which Tourist Board region each of these should be filed under.

b Why would you be having problems with the following brochures?

CRUISING THE INLAND WATERWAYS
ROMAN CITIES: BATH/YORK/CHESTER
DUBLIN CITY WEEKENDS

c Select one brochure which you might offer, and one which you would definitely not offer, to each of the following clients:
An elderly couple seeking a restful holiday.
A businesswoman planning to fly to New York.
A young couple with a two-year-old child.
A keen theatre and concert goer.

2 a Try to match up each of the places in List A, on page 45, with one of the attractions in List B.

List A	List B
York	The Beatles
Devon and Somerset	Snowdon Mountain Railway
North Wales	HMS Victory
London	The Jorvik Viking Museum
Birmingham	Loch Ness
Liverpool	Exmoor
Kent	The Tower and Illuminations
Portsmouth	British Museum
Blackpool	National Exhibition Centre
The Scottish Highlands	Dover Castle

b Now can you try and think of at least one more attraction in or near each of the List A places?

c Make a chart showing approximate distances and directions from your home to each of the List A places.

d Choose from the list the five places you would most like to visit. Write simple but clear instructions on how to get to each place from your home. You could use road (and motorway) routes for some journeys and rail or even air routes for others. Use a road atlas and British Rail system map to help you. List road/motorway numbers, mention towns you pass through or where you change trains or buses.

3 Compile some notes about the Isle of Wight, the Isle of Man, the Channel Islands and the Isle of Skye by deciding which of the following statements applies to each one and then writing the statements out under the correct island heading.

a Just off the south coast of England.

b In the middle of the Irish Sea.

c Separated by a narrow strait from the west coast of Scotland.

d Nearer to the coast of France than to Britain.

e Reached by ferries from Liverpool, Belfast, Dublin and Heysham.

f Cars usually cross between Kyle of Lochalsh and Kyleakin.

g Frequent ferries, hydrofoils and hovercraft run from Portsmouth, Lymington and Southampton.

h Both main islands are served by car ferries from Portsmouth and other south coast ports.

i Being the most southerly of the islands the mildest climate is experienced and there is plenty of sunshine.

j Exposed to the westerly winds and lying furthest north, it is wet but not too cold.

k As in neighbouring Ireland, Wales and Cumbria, there is plenty of rain.

l Sandown, Shanklin, Ventnor and Ryde are the main resorts.

m Douglas is the principal resort.

n St Helier and St Peter Port are the main towns on Jersey and Guernsey.

o Portree is the only town of any size.

p Spring flowers and glasshouse tomatoes are well-known island produce.

q Cowes Week attracts sailing enthusiasts from all over the world.

r The tough mountain course provides spectacular motor cycle racing.

s Climbers head for the peaks of the Cuillin Hills.

4 Make a list of features similar to that above which could describe the following places:

York
Cambridge
Windsor
Brighton.

5 Suggest a suitable tour, lasting about two weeks, for the following visitors to Britain. Work out the best order in which the places on the tour could be visited and the number of nights to be spent at each place and ensure that the tours start and end at one of the London airports. Give any special notes about transport, routes, etc. which might be useful.

a Wildlife and bird watching enthusiast.

b Someone keen to learn more of British history.

c Person keen to see major sporting locations.

6 Information to help you answer the following questions can be found on pages 48–50.

a You are to stay in the Apollo Hotel, Birmingham. Write down details of the route you will follow after leaving the M42. Give road numbers, junctions, landmarks etc.

b Complete the following description of the location of the Apollo Hotel using some of the words beneath the passage to fill in the gaps.

The hotel stands beside the A_____ road which leads _____wards from the major junction known as _____ Ways in Birmingham. It is at the junction of Hagley Road with Rotton Park Road. _____ Road, from which the car park can be reached, runs just behind the hotel. There is easy access to the _____ and M6 motorways while rail travellers are served by _____ Street Station and Birmingham International _____ is easily reached to the _____ of the city.

M5	M4	M25	north	south	east	west	47
456	45	Five	Three	York	Norfolk	Suffolk	
Old	New	Airport					

c From Birmingham you decide to visit Worcester.

  (i) How far is it from Birmingham?

  (ii) Which motorway will you use and which junction will be the most convenient, starting from the Apollo Hotel?

  (iii) On what waterways does Worcester stand?

  (iv) You plan to meet a friend who is to catch the 09.00 train from London to Worcester. What is the name of the station in Worcester and at about what time will your friend arrive there?

  (v) Which is the main pedestrianised shopping street in Worcester?

  (vi) Describe an important building found in the same street.

  (vii) What important building stands on the east bank of the river near the town centre?

d Another day out from Birmingham is spent exploring the area in and around Dudley.

  (i) Certain features are shown both on the Dudley area map and on the Birmingham/Apollo Hotel map. Which features are these?

  (ii) Explain the route you will take from the Apollo Hotel to Dudley.

  (iii) List the attractions to be seen in and around Dudley. Can you explain why the museum is called the 'Black Country' Museum? Three attractions have 'Crystal' in their name. Do you know what sort of industry these places represent? (Did you notice a related industry during your visit to Worcester?)

  (iv) Several forms of transport are mentioned or shown on the map. What can you say about the age of each type of transport—which came first and which is the most recent?

e With two days left of your visit to Birmingham you decide to spend one day in Birmingham itself and then to make one more excursion to somewhere of historical interest not too far away. Suggest a suitable place to visit and say what you will expect to see there.

f You plan to leave your hired car in Birmingham and go by train to Brighton. The British Rail Enquiry Office tell you that there is no need to go via London and change because there are through trains to Brighton.

  (i) Give the times of the direct trains from Birmingham New Street to Brighton. Why would one of them not be very convenient for most people?

  (ii) At which other Birmingham station could you catch these trains?

  (iii) You need to be in Brighton by 6 p.m. How much time will you have to spare if you catch the 14.05 from New Street?

  (iv) Where did this train start its journey and at which other stations did it stop before reaching Birmingham?

  (v) Will you be able to get a hot meal served to you on the train?

  (vi) On which days of the week does your train run?

Fig. 24 The Apollo Hotel, Birmingham

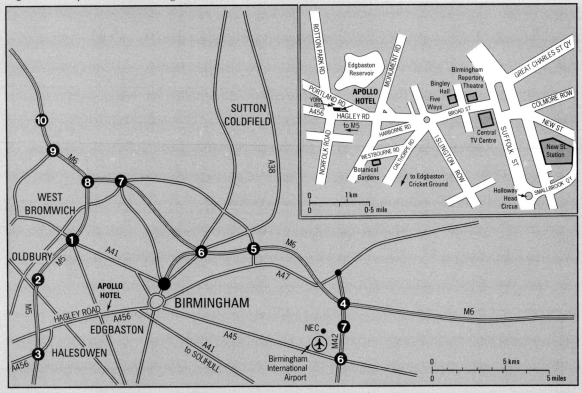

Fig. 25 British Rail timetable

The Northwest—Midlands—The Southeast

Manchester—Liverpool—Stoke—Birmingham—Coventry—via London Kensington Olympia—Gatwick Airport—Brighton—Newhaven—Folkestone—Dover

Mondays to Saturdays

		A		w		w	yw
Manchester Piccadilly			0644	0725d	0925	1215	1615
Stockport			0654	0733g	0933	1223	1623
Liverpool Lime Street			0625	0749	0900	1200	1605
Runcorn			0642	0806	0917	1217	1625
Crewe			0712	0832		1243	
Macclesfield			0708	0746	0948	1235	1635
Stoke-on-Trent			0730	0806	1008	1255	1700
Stafford			0753	0854	1029	1319	1723
Wolverhampton	0520					1337	
Sandwell & Dudley						1347	
Birmingham New Street	0539					1405	
Birmingham International	0548					1415	
Coventry	0559					1429	
Rugby	0622		0828				
Milton Keynes Central	0650		0951	1127			1821
Watford Junction	0716		0915	1014	1156	1530	1843
Kensington Olympia	0750	0803	0947	1047	1230	1602	1915
Clapham Junction	0802		0957			1614	1928
East Croydon	0817		1010			1627	1949p
Redhill						1642	2003s
Gatwick Airport	0834		1027			1653	2013v
Haywards Heath							2029x
Brighton	0858		1058n			1723	2114
Newhaven Harbour (Marine)							2115
Bromley South		0833h		1114	1257		
Tonbridge		0859k		1138	1320		
Ashford		0926		1204	1348		
Folkestone Central		0942		1219	1404		
Folkestone Harbour				1240			
Dover Western Docks		0954		1230	1415		

A   From Reading **0726**, Slough **0742**.
d   0730 Saturdays
g   **0741** Saturdays
h   **0827** Saturdays
w   Waiter service of hot dishes to 1st Class ticket holders only.
k   0856 Saturdays
n   1055 Saturdays
p   1942 Saturdays
s   1957 Saturdays
v   2010 Saturdays
x   2026 Saturdays
y   Catering to Gatwick

Light printing timings indicate connecting service.

Fig. 26 *Worcester*

WORCESTER

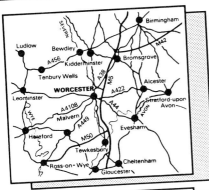

GETTING THERE IS EASY

RAIL
There are regular trains from Paddington, London to Shrub Hill, Worcester. The journey takes approximately two and a quarter hours.

ROAD
Excellent road links (leave M5 at Junction 7) 113 miles from London, 27 from Birmingham, 57 from Oxford, 25 from Cheltenham and 26 miles from Stratford-upon-Avon.

BOAT
The City stands on the banks of the River Severn and the Worcester – Birmingham canal. Free mooring is readily available.

INTERESTING BUILDINGS

Guildhall
High Street—one of the finest 18th century Guildhalls in England.

City Museum and Art Gallery
Foregate Street, including the colourful Worcester Regiment collection.

The Tudor House Museum
Exhibition displays of the social and domestic life of the City.

Elgar Birthplace Museum
Just 3 miles outside Worcester, a fascinating and atmospheric museum devoted to England's greatest composer.

Greyfriars
Friar Street—Mediaeval timber frame house (National Trust).

SHOPPING

The excellent shopping centre is now extensively pedestrianised, with superbly restored traditional shopping arcades.

Fig. 27 Dudley

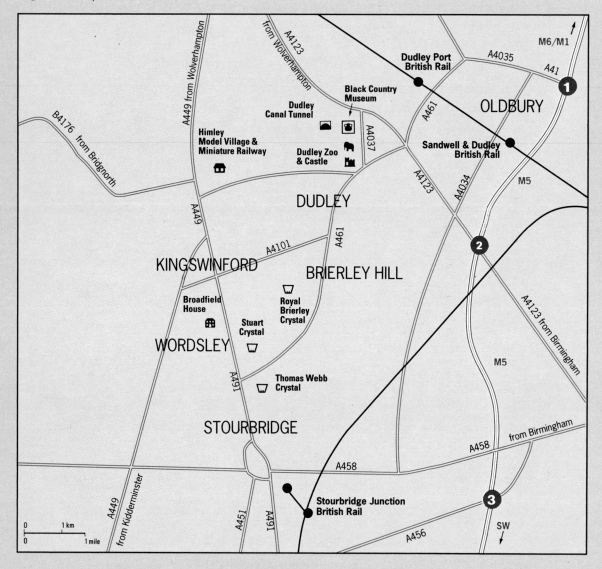

HOLIDAYS FURTHER AFIELD

7 *Travelling to Norway*

   a Look at the sailing schedule for 'MS Jupiter' on page 51 (Fig. 28).

   (i) From which port in England does the ship sail for Norway?

   (ii) If you were travelling in July, on which days of the week does the ship sail to Stavanger and Bergen?

   (iii) On which day does it sail direct to Bergen?

   (iv) How long does it take to get from England to Bergen via Stavanger?

   (v) How much quicker is the direct journey to Bergen?

Fig. 28 *Sailing schedule for MS Jupiter*

MS JUPITER
SCHEDULE 1989

NEWCASTLE / STAVANGER / BERGEN
March 18 — May 7 & Sept 9 — Dec 17

Dep Newcastle	Arr/Dep Stavanger	Arr Bergen
Tue 19.00	Wed 14.30/15.00	Wed 21.00
Sat 18.30	Sun 14.30/15.00	Sun 21.00

May 22 — Sept 7

Dep Newcastle	Arr/Dep Stavanger	Arr Bergen
Mon 16.00	Tue 11.00/11.30	Tue 17.00
Wed 18.30	Thur 14.30/15.00 ⟶	Thur 21.00
Sat 13.30		Sun 11.30

BERGEN / STAVANGER / NEWCASTLE
March 16 — May 5 & Sep 11 — Dec 15

Dep Bergen	Arr/Dep Stavanger	Arr Newcastle
Thur 17.00	Thur 23.00/23.30	Fri 17.00
Mon 11.30	Mon 17.30/18.00	Tue 12.00

May 21 — Sept 9

Dep Bergen	Arr/Dep Stavanger	Arr Newcastle
Tue 19.30	⟶	Wed 16.00
Fri 11.00	Fri 16.45/17.30	Sat 11.00
Sun 14.00	Sun 20.00/20.30	Mon 13.30

(vi) If you arrived in Bergen at 11.30 on Sunday, 1st July and wanted to spend a minimum of ten full days in Norway, when would be the next available return ferry from Bergen back to England? At what time would this ferry dock at the British port?

b Use maps and timetables to work out how you would get from your home to the departure port in time to catch the sailings mentioned in a (vi) above. Will you need overnight accommodation *en route*? If you plan to use public transport, remember to check that the service operates on the two days concerned. (Which days are these?)

c Consider whether there are any alternative ways of getting from where you live to Norway which would be easier or more convenient.

SIGHTSEEING IN EUROPE

You are working as a clerk in the Whistlestop Travel Agency. Your clients are a young couple on holiday from the United States and now that they have finished their tour of Britain they want to spend a fortnight in Europe seeing some of the best scenery and most famous cities.

8 Draw up your own list of places you think the couple should try to visit. Next, see if you can arrange them in a sensible order and suggest how they might travel from place to place.

As it turns out, they already have a good idea of what they want to see and are asking for advice about the route and for any helpful suggestions you can make to help them get the best out of their tour. Their list is as follows:

Cities	Other sights
AMSTERDAM	THE ALPS
PARIS	RIVER RHINE
ZURICH	DUTCH BULBFIELDS

9 Arrange these six destinations into a sensible order for their visit. (See answers section before continuing.)

10 You manage to find among the brochures and reference books in the Whistlestop Agency's files, all the information shown on pages 54–57. Use this material, and your own reference sources, to carry out the following tasks.

   a What is the name of the international airport near Amsterdam?

   b How can the couple travel between the airport and the city centre? What are the costs and times involved?

   c If they choose to travel from the airport by train, which hotel is nearest to the station and what will it cost for two people for three nights?

   d Which hotel is the cheapest within about a quarter of a mile of the station?

   e The travellers decide to stay at the cheapest hotel and as near the station as possible. Which of the two £17-a-night hotels do they choose?

   f Work out a route which will take them to all the main tourist attractions and back to their hotel. List the attractions in the order they will visit them.

You tell your clients that they will be able to book an excursion from Amsterdam to see the Dutch bulbfields.

   g (i) What arrangement is provided in the Rhine Cruise to Switzerland details for your clients to join the ship from Amsterdam?
       (ii) Where will they join the ship?

   h During the first night the ship crosses the border between which two countries?

i If they join the Tuesday departure, on what day will they pass the Lorelei Rock?

j Why might some of the passengers not be on the ship between Gernsheim and Speyer?

k On day 4 of the cruise there is a different country on each bank of the river. Which country is on which side?

l What supplement will your clients have to pay if they want a cabin like the one shown in the plan, on the Rhineland Deck?

m What currency should you advise the couple to take with them for buying drinks on board the ship?

From Basle station your clients will be able to catch a train to Zurich where they can stay for a few days and visit the Alps.

n Which of the tours shown on the Swiss map will allow them to see the most Alpine scenery?

o (i) If they take the three-day tour leaving Zurich on Monday morning, work out on which day of the week and in which towns they will spend their nights on the tour.
(ii) On what day and at what time will they arrive back in Zurich?

p The couple had planned to fly back to Paris and then to London but you suggest they try the Orient Express instead. Work out whether or not they will be in Zurich on the right day and at the right time to catch the train to Paris.

q What meals would they be able to have during the train journey? Can you see a reason why they might decide not to have one of these meals?

r Assuming that their stay in Amsterdam was for three nights, work out how much time they have left out of the fortnight they planned to stay in Europe.

s They can afford a 3-star hotel in Paris and decide either to stay as near as possible to the station where their train will arrive or nearer the centre. Suggest suitable hotels in each case.

t They ask you what they can see in Paris during their short stay. Although they have heard of most of the tourist attractions, the only one they know anything about is the Eiffel Tower. Find out about some of the other interesting sights marked on the Paris map and write brief details ready to give to your clients.

u How long will their journey from Paris to London take?

v The couple are concerned about the sea crossing and want to know which ferry route they will be using and about how long the crossing will take. Can you find out for them?

w What will be their final meal on their journey and where will they be when it is served?

x In what important way will the journey from Paris to London be different after about 1993?

Fig. 29 *Amsterdam*

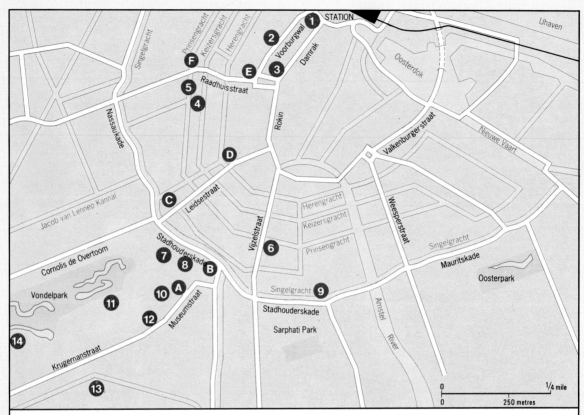

To and from the Airport

Taxi - readily available. Cost from Amsterdam approx. £14.00 and they will carry up to 4 passengers. Journey time approx. 30 min.

Train - a direct service every 15 min. from Central Station to Schiphol Airport. Cost approx. £1.40. Journey time 20 min.

HOTELS

1 Holiday Inn
2 Pullman
3 Krasnapolsky
4 De Gouden Kettingh
5 Pulitzer
6 Arthur Frommer
7 Park
8 Museum
9 Nicolaas Witsen
10 Acca
11 Atlas
12 Trianon
13 Hilton
14 Borgmann

TOURIST ATTRACTIONS

A Van Gogh Museum
B Rijksmuseum
C Leidseplein
D Flower Market
E Dam Square
F Anne Frank House

Hotels in Amsterdam (Price does not include breakfast)	£ per night
Nicolaas Witsen	£ 17
De Gouden Kettingh	£ 17
Borgmann	£ 18
Arthur Frommer	£ 19
Atlas	£ 19
Museum & Trianon	£ 19
Park	£ 19
Acca	£ 20
Pullman	£ 21
Krasnapolsky	£ 23
Pulitzer	£ 23
Hilton	£ 23
Holiday Inn	£ 24

Fig. 30 Rhine cruise to Switzerland

Rhine Cruise to Switzerland

Start your holiday with a leisurely cruise up the River Rhine from Holland

With this cruise the journey is very much part of your holiday as you progress at a leisurely pace up the great River Rhine. The scenery drifts slowly by with a constantly changing landscape throughout the day whilst on board you will be offered excellent food and service. There are some interesting optional excursions to be made during the voyage and of course plenty of time to relax on the sun decks.

THE PRICE INCLUDES:

* Transfers from Amsterdam Airport direct to Nijmegen.

* Accommodation on board for four nights.

* Four meals daily: Breakfast , lunch and dinner plus afernoon tea, from dinner on Day One to lunch on Day Five.

* Transfer from Landing Stage in Basle to the station for the train for the onward journey to your holiday resort.

The ships which are operated by KD Rhine Line, carry up to 200 passengers and all have Dining Room, Bar, Observation Lounge, Shop, Reading Room and Veranda. They each have Sun Deck and a covered Leisure Deck and some have a small swimming pool. All cabins have outside windows and are comfortably appointed. The German Mark is used on board and there is a Bureau de Change. The optional excursions during the cruise can be booked on board.

The price is £356 per person. This includes a two berth cabin (Cabin Type A2) with upper and lower berth plus shower and w.c. For a double cabin with two lower berths (plus shower and w.c.) on the Rhineland Deck (Cabin Type A1) there is a supplement of £109 per person or £145 on the Loreley Deck. Single cabin add £109.

Reductions for Children (Age 2-11)
Children occupying own cabin - 45% .
Extra berth in a 2 berth cabin - 70% Reduction

CRUISE PROGRAMME

Day One (Sat or Tues)
A private transfer is provided from Amsterdam to Nijmegen where you board the Rhine Steamer. You settle in to your cabin and then after dinner you are invited by the Captain to his "Welcome Reception" with music and dancing.

Day Two
By 09.00 the ship has arrived at the famous German cathedral city of Cologne. The ship spends three hours here and an escorted sightseeing visit of Cologne is available. At noon the cruise continues on past Bonn (Germany's Capital City). Königswinter and Koblenz to Braubach where you arrive at 20.30. A visit can be made this evening to the famous castle at Marksburg.

Day Three
The ship leaves Braubach in the early morning and today's scenery is a constant succession of castles, vineyards and little riverside towns. You also pass the famous Lorelei Rock the home of the "spirits" of the Rhine. The ship makes a brief stop at Gernsheim and there is the opportunity of a visit to the famous old University town of Heidelberg with a farmer's dinner, music, dancing and entertainment. If you take this excursion you rejoin the ship at Speyer at about 22.30.

Day Four
During the night the ship leaves for the next stage of the cruise and now you have France on one side of you and The Black Forest on the other. At 15.00 you reach the French city of Strasbourg with its great gothic cathedral and picturesque "Old Town". The ship stays here for the evening and an escorted excursion of Strasbourg is available.

Day Five
The final stage of the cruise takes you along the Rhine Canal and before lunch there is the Captain's "Farewell Reception". Arrival in the Swiss City of Basle is at 15.00. After disembarkation you are transferred to Basle Station.

Fig. 31 *The Glacier Express*

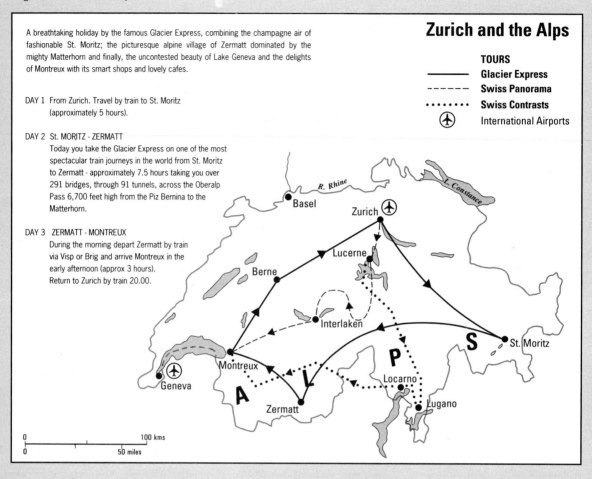

A breathtaking holiday by the famous Glacier Express, combining the champagne air of fashionable St. Moritz; the picturesque alpine village of Zermatt dominated by the mighty Matterhorn and finally, the uncontested beauty of Lake Geneva and the delights of Montreux with its smart shops and lovely cafes.

DAY 1 From Zurich. Travel by train to St. Moritz (approximately 5 hours).

DAY 2 St. MORITZ - ZERMATT
Today you take the Glacier Express on one of the most spectacular train journeys in the world from St. Moritz to Zermatt - approximately 7.5 hours taking you over 291 bridges, through 91 tunnels, across the Oberalp Pass 6,700 feet high from the Piz Bernina to the Matterhorn.

DAY 3 ZERMATT - MONTREUX
During the morning depart Zermatt by train via Visp or Brig and arrive Montreux in the early afternoon (approx 3 hours). Return to Zurich by train 20.00.

Zurich and the Alps

TOURS
— **Glacier Express**
- - - **Swiss Panorama**
······ **Swiss Contrasts**
✈ International Airports

Fig. 32 *Switzerland—London*

SWITZERLAND - LONDON

Every Wednesday and Saturday from 16 March to 16 November.

Buchs
Zürich   dep.21.00
Paris (Gare de Lyon)   dep.23.57
London (Victoria Station)   arr 09.08
                                          arr. 18.34

Meals Included
Supper between Zürich and Paris
Continental breakfast in your cabin prior to arrival in Paris.
Brunch between Paris and Boulogne.
Afternoon tea between Folkestone and London.

Fig. 33 *Paris—Hotels and principal tourist attractions*

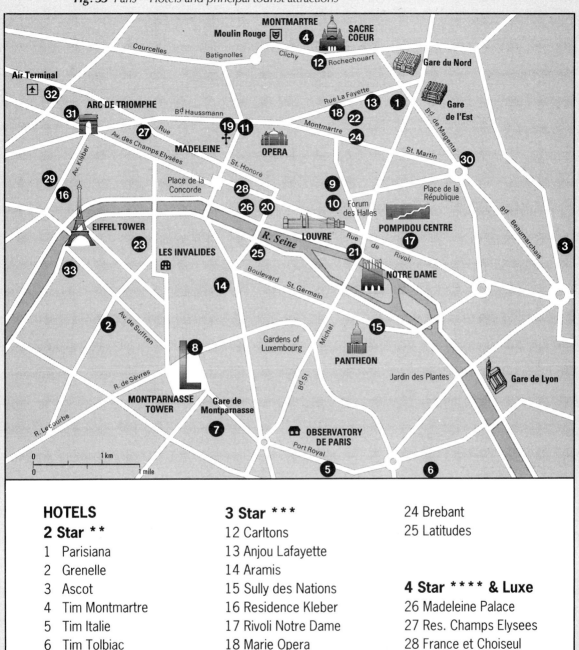

HOTELS
2 Star * *

1 Parisiana
2 Grenelle
3 Ascot
4 Tim Montmartre
5 Tim Italie
6 Tim Tolbiac
7 Tim Maine
8 Tim Montparnasse
9 Tim La Bourse
10 Tim Le Louvre
11 Tim St. Lazare

3 Star * * *

12 Carltons
13 Anjou Lafayette
14 Aramis
15 Sully des Nations
16 Residence Kleber
17 Rivoli Notre Dame
18 Marie Opera
19 Newton Opera
20 Res. La Concorde
21 Britannique
22 Corona
23 Jardins d'Eiffel

24 Brebant
25 Latitudes

4 Star * * * * & Luxe

26 Madeleine Palace
27 Res. Champs Elysees
28 France et Choiseul
29 Garden Elysee
30 Holiday Inn
31 Splendid Etoile
32 Meridien Etoile
33 Hilton

A WORLD CRUISE

11 The luxury cruise liner 'Canberra' leaves Southampton on the evening of Monday, 8th January on a round-the-world cruise which will end back in Southampton on April 9th. The full schedule is shown below and on page 59 there is a map showing the whole route.

Fig. 34 *Canberra World Cruise Schedule 1990*

CANBERRA WORLD CRUISE 1990

SOUTHAMPTON
Mon 8 Jan evening sailing

MADEIRA
Fri 12 Jan arr 8.30am dep 6.30pm

BERMUDA*
Wed 17 Jan arr 8.00am. Dep 6.00am Thu 18 Jan

FORT LAUDERDALE - U.S.A.
Sat 20 Jan arr 7.30am dep 6.30pm

MONTEGO BAY* - Jamaica
Mon 22 Jan arr 8.30am dep 6.30pm

BONAIRE - Dutch Antilles
Wed 24 Jan arr 7.30am dep 7.00pm

BALBOA - Panama
Fri 26 Jan arr 4.00pm dep Midnight

ACAPULCO* - Mexico
Tue 30 Jan arr 7.30am dep 7.30pm

SAN FRANCISCO - U.S.A.
Sat 3 Feb arr 8.00am. Dep 1.00am Sun 4 Feb

HONOLULU - Hawaii
Thu 8 Feb arr 8.00am dep Midnight

LAUTOKA - Fiji
Thu 15 Feb arr 9.00am dep 7.00pm

AUCKLAND - New Zealand
Sun 18 Feb arr 7.30am dep 9.00pm

SYDNEY - Australia
Wed 21 Feb arr 7.00am. Dep 6.00pm Thu 22 Feb

HONIARA* - Solomon Islands
Mon 26 Feb arr 7.30am dep 6.30pm

RABAUL* - Papua New Guinea
Wed 28 Feb arr 7.30am dep 7.00pm

KEELUNG (for Taipei) - Taiwan
Mon 5 Mar arr 9.00am dep Midnight

HONG KONG
Wed 7 Mar arr 7.00am. Dep 2.00am Fri 9 Mar

PATTAYA* (for Bangkok) - Thailand
Mon 12 Mar arr 6.30am. Dep 7.00pm Tue13 Mar

SINGAPORE
Thu 15 Mar arr 9.00am. Dep 1.00pm Fri 16 Mar

PORT KELANG (for Kuala Lumpur) - Malaysia
Sat 17 Mar arr 7.30am dep 6.30pm

BOMBAY* - India
Thu 22 Mar arr 8.00am dep 10.00pm

AQABA - Jordan
Wed 28 Mar arr 8.00am dep 7.30pm

SUEZ* - Egypt
Thu 29 Mar arr 8.00pm. Dep 6.00am Fri 30 Mar

PORT SAID (for Cairo & the Pyramids) - Egypt
Fri 30 Mar arr 7.00pm. Dep 9.30pm Sat 31 Mar

ATHENS* - Greece
Mon 2 Apr arr 7.30am dep 8.00pm

NAPLES - Italy
Wed 4 Apr arr 7.30am dep Midnight

SOUTHAMPTON
Mon 9 Apr arr early morning

* Land by launch or tender

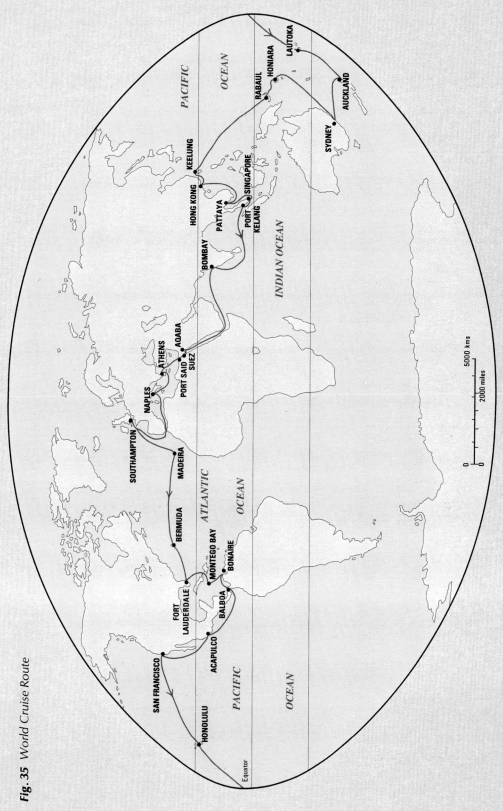

Fig. 35 World Cruise Route

a Which island will you pass as you sail out of Southampton?

b Which ocean is crossed between Madeira and Bermuda?

c How many days does this crossing take?

d By what means does the ship pass through Central America and into the Pacific Ocean?

e Name two ports on the west coast of North America where the 'Canberra' will call.

f What important line of latitude will the ship cross before reaching Honolulu?

g Between which ports will the liner cross the Equator?

h In which country will passengers find themselves when the ship docks at Auckland?

i How long will the ship spend in Sydney Harbour? Suggest one famous sight to be seen there.

j Name the two large and famous seaports in the Far East which will be visited on this cruise.

k Which port, and which country, will passengers visit on Thursday, 22nd March?

l Name the ocean crossed after leaving this port.

m As the 'Canberra' sails through the Red Sea towards Aqaba and Suez, which ancient country will passengers be able to see from the port (left-hand) side of the ship?

n After passing through the Suez Canal, what sea will the ship enter?

o Near the mouth of which major river will the ship be as it enters Port Said?

p On passage to Athens the 'Canberra' will pass close to a long, narrow island belonging to Greece. Name this island.

q To reach Naples by the shortest route the ship will sail through the narrow Strait of Messina. The 'toe' of mainland Italy will be on the right. Which large island will passengers see to the left?

r Put into the correct order the following countries and other geographical features which the ship will pass on the final leg of the voyage back to Southampton:

ESTORIL   THE BALEARIC ISLANDS   LAND'S END

GIBRALTAR   COSTA DEL SOL   THE ALGARVE   THE NEEDLES

s Work out the best route from Southampton back to your home.

Answers to Chapter 6

Some of the questions depend on opinions and ideas while the answers to others vary depending on where you live. Only parts of questions where clear answers can be given are included here.

1 a *THE ENGLISH LAKES*—Cumbria
THE ISLE OF WIGHT—Southern
ANTRIM AND GIANT'S CAUSEWAY—Northern Ireland
THE EDINBURGH FESTIVAL—Scotland
SHAKESPEARE COUNTRY—Heart of England
BOATING ON THE BROADS—East Anglia
CANTERBURY AND THE CINQUE PORTS—South East
WEEKENDS IN OXFORD—Thames and Chilterns
CLIMBING IN THE CAIRNGORMS—Scotland
SPECTACULAR SKYE—Scotland
HEATHROW HOTELS—London
LINCOLNSHIRE BULBFIELDS COACH TOUR—East Midlands
TORQUAY: THE ENGLISH RIVIERA—South West

b Inland Waterways and Roman Cities—cannot be filed because they cover more than one Tourist Board region.
Dublin—not in Great Britain (Irish Republic).

c Elderly couple: Lincolnshire Bulbfields ✓ Cairngorms ✗
Businesswoman: Heathrow Hotels ✓ Isle of Wight ✗
Young couple: Torquay ✓ The Edinburgh Festival ✗
Theatre/concert goer: Shakespeare Country ✓ The Broads ✗
(There are several alternative answers—in some cases you would need to have more detailed information. Not all young couples with children want to sit on the beach all day!)

2 a

LIST A	LIST B
York	The Jorvik Viking Museum
Devon and Somerset	Exmoor
North Wales	Snowdon Mountain Railway
London	British Museum
Birmingham	National Exhibition Centre
Liverpool	The Beatles
Kent	Dover Castle
Portsmouth	HMS Victory
Blackpool	The Tower and Illuminations
The Scottish Highlands	Loch Ness

b Many alternatives, e.g.:
York—National Railway Museum
Devon/Somerset—Coastal Path
North Wales—Slate Quarries
London—St Paul's Cathedral
Birmingham—Black Country Museum
Liverpool—Albert Dock
Kent—Canterbury Cathedral
Portsmouth—the Mary Rose exhibition
Blackpool—Pleasure Beach
Scottish Highlands—Aviemore

3 Key to answers: W = Isle of Wight; M = Isle of Man; C = Channel Islands; S = Isle of Skye

a W	**h** C	**n** C
b M	**i** C	**o** S
c S	**j** S	**p** C
d C	**k** M	**q** W
e M	**l** W	**r** M
f S	**m** M	**s** S
g W		

4 There are many possible answers but the following provide some ideas:
York: Ancient city with famous Minster and city walls. Now home to National Railway Museum and Viking Museum. Has a race course.
Cambridge: Ancient University city in flat fen country of East Anglia. The River Cam flows past the colleges and close to King's College Chapel.

Windsor: This town is dominated by its castle where the Royal family are frequent visitors. The River Thames flows through the town and Eton College is just across the bridge from Windsor.

Brighton: Fashionable Regency town and holiday resort on the Sussex coast. Easily reached (50 miles) from London, it has two piers, a large yachting marina, an Indian-style Pavilion and is used for major conferences.

5 There are too many possibilities for answers to be provided but do note the following points.

There are many 'special interest' holiday packages available. Because individual people's needs vary so much, you would need to enquire in more detail—the wildlife enthusiast would probably know where the best sites were and would need help in travel and accommodation arrangements, the historian could tell you which aspects of history were of most interest and the sports person could indicate whether golf or tennis, horse-racing or athletics, soccer or cricket were of most interest.

6 **a** Driving north on M42 leave motorway at junction 6 and take A45 towards Birmingham city centre. (You will pass Birmingham Airport on the right soon after leaving the motorway.) In the city centre you will need to look for Broad Street (the turning next to the Central TV Centre and Repertory Theatre). At the other end of Broad Street is a big junction called Five Ways. Take the A456 (called Hagley Road) from here and the Apollo Hotel is on the right, just before you get to Norfolk Road.

b The hotel stands beside the *A456* road which leads *west*wards from the major junction known as *Five* Ways in Birmingham. It is at the junction of Hagley Road with Rotton Park Road. *York* Road, from which the car park can be reached, runs just behind the hotel. There is easy access to the *M5* and M6 motorways while rail travellers are served by *New* Street Station and Birmingham International *Airport* is easily reached to the *east* of the city.

c (i) 27 miles.

(ii) M5, junction 3.

(iii) River Severn and Worcester–Birmingham Canal.

(iv) Shrub Hill Station; arrive about 11.15.

(v) High Street.

(vi) The Guildhall—fine 18th Century building.

(vii) The Cathedral.

d (i) M5 motorway, Junctions 1–3; Oldbury; A456 road.

(ii) Along A456 Hagley Road to Halesowen, turn right towards Oldbury, across M5 motorway at Jc.2 then left on to A461 towards Dudley Zoo and Castle.

(iii) All the attractions are shown on the map. The 'Black Country' name came from the days when this was a heavy industrial area with many factories burning coal and creating a grimy, black environment. The area is much changed today. Crystal is connected with glassware manufacture. There is a famous porcelain factory in Worcester.

(iv) The oldest transport shown would be some of the roads which were originally used by horses. Next came the canals, then railways and, most recently, motorways.

e Many places to choose from including Stratford-on-Avon, Warwick Castle, the Ironbridge Gorge, etc.

f (i) 05.39 and 14.05. First is too early for most people.

(ii) Birmingham International.

(iii) 37 minutes if the train is on time.

(iv) Yes—but only if you travel 1st class.

(v) Mondays to Saturdays—not Sundays.

7 **a** (i) From Newcastle.

(ii) Monday and Wednesday.

(iii) Saturday.

(iv) Between 25 and $26\frac{1}{2}$ hours.

(v) Three or four hours quicker (about 22 hrs).

(vi) Friday at 11.00 (10 days expires at 11.30 on Wednesday).

8 The list could be very long. A fortnight is a very short time in which to see one country, let alone a continent.

9 Three of the places are geographically connected—Amsterdam is close to the bulbfields and the Rhine enters the North Sea not far away. The Rhine also flows from the Alps and Zurich is not far from the Alps. Paris is very easily reached by air or overland from almost anywhere in

Europe. You could have suggested flying to Zurich, touring the Alps, taking a Rhine cruise ending in Holland and then a trip to Paris before flying home. Alternatively the tour could have started with Paris, then by train or plane to Zurich and the Alps, ending with the Rhine and Holland. Several other variants are possible. The important thing is that you should be able to visualise where these places are and be able to plan logically for the journeys. Your answers to question 10 assume that the chosen order is Amsterdam (and excursion to bulbfields), Rhine Cruise to Basle (and train to Zurich), Alpine tour returning to Zurich, by Orient Express train to Paris and then continuing to Britain.

10 a Schiphol.
  b Taxi—30 minutes, £14 for two (only £7 if two more people share the cost!).
  Train—20 minutes, £2.80 for two.
  c Holiday Inn—2 × 24 × 3 = £144.
  d The Pullman is within a quarter mile and costs £21.
  e The De Gouden Kettingh is nearest the station.
  f Several alternatives possible—perhaps best to walk to the more distant attraction first (the Van Gogh Museum) and finishing at Anne Frank House, close to the hotel.
  g (i) A 'private transfer' (meaning a coach or car) to...
  (ii) Nijmegen.
  h The Netherlands (Holland) and West Germany.
  i Thursday.
  j They could have taken the excursion to Heidelberg while the ship sails between these two points.
  k France is on the right, Germany on the left (facing forward).
  l £109 each (Cabin type is A1).
  m German Marks.
  n Glacier Express.
  o (i) Monday night in St Moritz, Tuesday in Zermatt.
  (ii) Wednesday at 20.00.
  p Their timing is perfect for the Orient Express—it leaves on Wednesday night at 23.57.

  q Supper and breakfast (but midnight is rather late for eating supper!).
  r They have used time as follows:
  Amsterdam—3 nights
  Rhine cruise—4 nights
  Glacier Express—2 nights
  Orient Express—1 night
  Ten nights (11 days) so far, so they can stay two or three nights in Paris.
  s Hotel nos 15, 17 or 21 are near the Gare de Lyon; no. 19 is very central—but there are others and the tourist attractions in Paris are quite spread out.
  t You will need to consult a guide book—but it is important to be able to distinguish between different kinds of attraction—the Louvre and the Folies-Bergère, for example!
  u Almost 12 hours (but remember time differences—French time is usually one hour ahead of British).
  v Boulogne to Folkstone—about 1½ hours.
  w Afternoon tea between Folkstone and London.
  x The Channel Tunnel is scheduled to open in 1993 making it possible to travel from Paris to London by direct train.

11 a Isle of Wight.
  b Atlantic.
  c About 5½ days.
  d The Panama Canal.
  e Acapulco and San Francisco.
  f The Tropic of Cancer.
  g Honolulu and Lautoka.
  h New Zealand.
  i Two days; Sydney Opera House and the Harbour Bridge.
  j Hong Kong and Singapore.
  k Bombay, India.
  l Indian Ocean.
  m Egypt.
  n The Mediterranean.
  o The Nile.
  p Crete.
  q Sicily.
  r Balearic Islands—Costa del Sol—Gibraltar—Algarve—Estoril—Land's End—The Needles.

Acknowledgements

The author and publishers are grateful to the following for permission to reproduce copyright material

Controller of Her Majesty's Stationery Office *pages* 1,2 (bottom), 3 (top)

Mary Evans Picture Library *page* 2 and cover

Britain on View (BTA/ETB) *page* 3 (bottom), 11

British Tourist Authority *pages* 6, 32

British Nuclear Fuels plc *page* 9

Countryside Commission *page* 13

Spanish National Tourist Office *page* 17

J. Schytte/The Danish Tourist Board *page* 22 and cover

Tom Hanley *page* 23

P. & P. F. James Ltd *pages* 27,33

CN Rail *page* 30 and cover

Brian Towler *page* 31 and cover

John Buttivant *page 35*

Caledonian MacBrayne Ltd *page* 38 (bottom)

Martin Rooks Holidays *page* 40

British Rail *page* 48 (bottom)

Canberra Cruises *pages* 58, 59

Maps by *Mike Shand*

Cover Illustration by *Stephen Jeffrey*